Arbeitsblätter

Englische Grammatik 7./8. Schuljahr

34 Arbeitsblätter
für einen kommunikativen Grammatikunterricht

von Detlef und Margaret von Ziegésar

Ernst Klett Schulbuchverlag Leipzig
Leipzig Stuttgart Düsseldorf

Abbildungsnachweise:
S. 9: linkes Foto: dpa
rechtes Foto: dpa Bajzat
(Deutsche Presseagentur GmbH)
S. 43: Daily Mirror, 22/7/87
S. 53: Ralf Doll Fotografie, Karlsbad

Bibliografische Information Der Deutschen Bibliothek
Die Deutsche Bibliothek verzeichnet diese Publikation in der Deutschen Nationalbibliografie; detaillierte bibliografische Daten sind im Internet über http://dnb.ddb.de abrufbar.

1. Auflage A 1 9 8 7 6 5 | 2007 2006 2005 2004 2003

Alle Drucke dieser Auflage können im Unterricht nebeneinander benutzt werden, sie sind untereinander unverändert. Die letzte Zahl bezeichnet das Jahr dieses Druckes.

Internetadresse: http://www.klett-verlag.de

Umschlaggestaltung: BSS Werbeagentur Sachse und Partner, Bietigheim
Illustrationen: Christa Janik, Leinfelden-Echterdingen
Druck und Bindung: Wilhelm Röck, Weinsberg
Printed in Germany.
ISBN 3-12-927875-3

Allgemeines

Dies ist das zweite von drei Arbeitsbüchern zur Übung und Wiederholung von Grammatikstrukturen im Englischunterricht der Sekundarstufe I. Der vorliegende zweite Band umfasst das Grammatikpensum der Klassen 7 und 8, der erste Band enthält die in den Klassen 5 und 6 behandelten Grammatikstrukturen, und der dritte Band übt und wiederholt das Grammatikpensum der Klassen 9 und 10.

Der erste Teil der einzelnen Bände enthält für jede behandelte Grammatikstruktur sorgfältig durchdachte und im Unterricht erprobte Arbeitsblätter. In einem Kommentarteil werden Hinweise zum Einsatz der Arbeitsblätter gegeben. Er enthält außerdem die entsprechenden Lösungen bzw. Lösungsvorschläge.

Die Arbeitsbücher können sowohl im Verbund mit einem Lehrwerk als auch lehrbuchunabhängig verwendet werden. Der Wortschatz sowie die Progressionen der grammatischen Strukturen korrespondieren mit denen der gängigen Englischlehrwerke.

Man kann die Arbeitsbücher in der vorgegebenen Reihenfolge der Strukturen systematisch durchgehen, aber auch je nach Bedarf einzelne Grammatikphänomene herausgreifen.

Die Arbeitsblätter enthalten sowohl mündliche als auch schriftliche Übungen und berücksichtigen die verschiedenen Sozialformen des Unterrichts. Dadurch ist der Einsatz der Arbeitsblätter vielfältig. Es gibt lehrergelenkte Übungen, Gruppen-, Partner- und Projektarbeit. Einzelarbeit ist sowohl in der Klasse als auch zu Hause in Form von Hausaufgaben möglich.

Grammatik

Der vorliegende Band übt und wiederholt die wichtigsten Grammatikphänomene der Klassen 7 und 8 mit strukturierten Materialien in Form von Arbeitsblättern.

Die Arbeitsblätter sind einerseits nach formalgrammatischen Gesichtspunkten geordnet und folgen damit der von den Lehrplänen der verschiedenen Bundesländer vorgeschriebenen und in Lehrwerken verwirklichten Strukturenprogression. Andererseits betten sie die zu übenden Grammatikstrukturen in natürliche Kommunikationsituationen ein und wählen den Strukturen angemessene Textsorten und Themen. Dadurch ist sowohl ein formalgrammatisches Üben und Einschleifen als auch ein kommunikatives Verwenden der Strukturen gewährleistet.

Obwohl der Schwerpunkt der Arbeitsblätter auf dem Üben und Wiederholen von Grammatikstrukturen liegt, werden immer wieder Gelegenheiten zum induktiven Erarbeiten von Grammatikregeln geboten. Regeln werden, wenn notwendig, in übersichtlichen Merkkästchen zusammengefasst. Die Regeln sind auf deutsch und in einer schülernahen Sprache verfasst, die den Lernenden vermittelt, dass Regeln nicht um ihrer selbst willen zu lernen sind, sondern als Hilfsmittel zum Erlernen der fremden Sprache.

Textsorten, Themen und Sozialformen

Soweit wie möglich wird mit sprachlich zwar vereinfachten, aber authentischen Textsorten gearbeitet. Es kommen informative Sachtexte vor, Erzähltexte, ein Comic, Fragebögen, Werbeplakate, Poster, Schlagzeilen aus Zeitungen und Statistiken. Die Schüler üben und wiederholen auf diese Weise Grammatikstrukturen mithilfe von Texten, die ihnen glaubwürdig erscheinen und denen sie in der Realität begegnen können.

Die Themen sind schülernah, indem sie die Erfahrungs- und Interessenlage der Lernenden berücksichtigen und damit die Bereitschaft der Schüler, sich mitzuteilen, nützen. Sie gehen nicht nur auf spezifisch landeskundliche Bereiche der Zielsprachekulturen ein, sondern sind auch von allgemeinem, fächerübergreifendem Interesse, wie z. B. die Themen Umwelt- und Verkehrsprobleme, Dritte Welt, Tourismus, Leben in der Wüste, Erfindungen, zwischenmenschliche Beziehungen und Zukunftsprognosen.

Schließlich beziehen die Themen interkulturelle Aspekte mit ein, wie z. B. Lebensweisen und -bedingungen in Ländern zusätzlich zu denen der Zielsprachekulturen, und fördern

damit Offenheit in der Begegnung mit Menschen anderer Herkunft.
Interkulturelle Kommunikationskompetenz im Sinne von uneigennützigem Fremdverstehen fängt aber schon im Umgang mit dem nächsten Schüler und beim Verhältnis der Schüler untereinander an. Deshalb wurden neben der Möglichkeit zur lehrerzentrierten und Einzelarbeit sozial-integrative Beziehungsformen wie Partner- und Gruppenarbeit gewählt, die neben dem kognitiven vor allem das soziale Lernen fördern, gleichzeitig die Sprechzeit der Lernenden beträchtlich erweitern und schließlich die Kommunikation wirklichen Wissens und realer Information mit wirklichen Kommunikationspartnern gewährleisten.
Die Begriffe „Schüler" und „Lehrer" werden im Folgenden als neutrale Sammelbezeichnungen verwendet, die jeweils beide Geschlechter umfassen.

Tourism – yes or no?

This village is very beautiful, but also very poor. The only money that people get is from fishing. Some people think that tourism would be good for the village. Others are not so sure. They are afraid it would change their way of life too much.
Some of the villagers are discussing the problem:

"If we don't do something our lives will never get better. Look at my shop here. If things don't change soon I'll have to close it. But if tourists come they'll buy more things and I'll be able to keep going."

"And they'll eat in our restaurants. How many people come to my restaurant? Maybe ten in a week! We'll have more money to buy things like cars. And we'll be able to build better houses."

"Of course. If we have more money life will be better for all of us. We'll be able to build a better school and a hospital. If we don't have tourists nothing will ever change."

"You're right. And what about the young people? Where will they find jobs?"
Others are not so happy about tourism. They have seen what has happened in other places.

"If tourists come they'll need hotels. And they'll want things like cinemas and discos."

"We'll need more car parks, too."

"But then there won't be much land left. And it will become more expensive. We won't be able to afford it."

"You're right. If the hotel owners buy all the land there won't be any for us. We'll have to move away. We won't able to live here any longer."

"And what about water? Tourists will want swimming pools. There's not much water now. If we have to build swimming pools there won't be enough water for all of us."

Unter einer bestimmten Bedingung wird etwas passieren. Wir verwenden:

für die Bedingung: **If + simple present**	für das, was passieren wird: **future**
If tourists **come**	we **will have** more money. there **will not** be enough water.
If tourists **don't come**	we **won't have** enough money.

Arguments for tourism

1. Fisherman: (more people/to be – to sell)
   If there *are* more people I *'ll sell* more fish.

2. Fisherman's wife: (not get – not have)
   If we ______________ more money we ______________ enough schools.

3. Woman selling things in market: (more people/to come – to sell)
   If ______________________ I ______________ more things.

4. Teenager without a job: (tourists/to come – to get a job)

____ in a hotel.

5. Café owner: (tourists/not come – have to)

____ close my café.

Arguments against tourism

Start each sentence with: *If…*

> *will not* = *won't* (gesprochene Sprache)

1. (tourists/to come – to need)

If ____________________ they ______________ hotels, shops and restaurants.

2. (to build – not be)

____ we __________ hotels, shops and car parks there ____________________ enough land for us.

3. (more people/to need – to get)

____________________________ land it ______________ more expensive.

4. (the land/to be – not be able to)

____________________ too expensive we ______________________ live here.

Can you go on? Write the sentences down in your exercise books.

If	tourists come	use a lot of water
	there are more tourists	be more cars
	more cars	the air – be dirtier
	tourists don't come	village stay clean and quiet
	have a tourist industry	the young people – not go fishing any more

Can you think of any more consequences?

If …

1. The world we live in

What kind of problems do these pictures show?
What could we do about them?

If there **weren't** so many cars
the air **would be** cleaner.

If we **recycled** more
we **wouldn't have** so much rubbish.

What do you think?

– *If*… the air *would* be cleaner.

use buses trams trains
two people – one car have
drive share electric solar

– We *wouldn't have* so much rubbish *if*…

buy packets plastic bags
collect cans bottles
use more than once

If there **weren't** so many cars **If** we **recycled** more	the air **would be** cleaner. we **wouldn't have** so much rubbish.
Für die **Bedingungen**, unter denen etwas passieren bzw. nicht passieren **würde:**	Für die vermeintliche **Folge:**
If + simple past	**would(n't) + Infinitiv**

2. How could we make the world a better place?

1. If we ________ bikes and buses more often there ________________ so many cars.
   (use – not be)

2. ____ there ______________ so many cars the air ________________ cleaner.
   (not be – be)

3. ____ we ____________ so many chemicals into the sea the water __________ cleaner.
   (not put – be)

4. It ________________ for the land, too, if we ______________ so many chemicals.
   (be better – not use)

Any more ideas?

– If we/people …

– It would be better if …

– We could save energy/water if …

– If we didn't …

1. What were they all doing?

Yesterday, sometime between four in the afternoon and midnight, two hundred videos were stolen from a shop. The police want to find out what all these people were doing at that time.

Police: What were you doing between four and six o'clock, Joe?

> Between four and six
> Joe **was** clean**ing** his bike.
>
> **Past continuous** für Handlungen, die zu einem **bestimmten** Zeitpunkt in der Vergangenheit gerade im Gang waren.

I **was** clean**ing** my bike.

And from six to eight? (learn to use)

And between eight and midnight? (have a drink)

What did Andy and Liz say?

Between four and six (wash the car)

From six to about seven (take the dog for a walk)

Between seven and twelve (dance at a party)

And Johnny?

Between four and six (paint the bathroom)

From six to seven (watch a film)

Between seven and twelve (play in a band)

And what about Donna and Tony?

From five to six (jog)

Between six and eight (watch a football match)

Who was not telling the truth?

2. What were you doing?

Make cards like this. Use the expressions below.

I phoned you three times yesterday between nine and eleven. Where were you?	*Sorry, I was visiting friends.*

I was (listening to music/playing football, the trumpet/having a bath/ riding my bike/hoovering the carpet/talking to someone outside/ helping … in the garden/ …)

Now ask your classmates:

Pupil 1: I phoned you three times yesterday between …
Where were you?
Pupil 2: I was … I phoned you three times yesterday between …
Where were you?
Pupil 3: I was … usw.

– Fred was very angry when somebody asked him to take his mask off at a party.
– Why?
– He wasn't wearing one.

1. Kevin's holiday

Kevin has just come back from a camping holiday. It was terrible.
Look what happened.

While he *was putting* his tent up it *rained.*

Someone __________ his radio while he ____________________ (steal/swim)

Warum hast du zwei verschiedene Zeiten verwendet?

Für eine Handlung in der Vergangenheit, die *unterbrochen* wurde, verwenden wir ____________________. Für die neu einsetzende Handlung ____________.

What else happened to Kevin? *while* – während

1. He __________ asleep (fall) while __________ ____________________ and got sunburned.

2. While ______________________________
he ______________________________

3. His dog __________ away __________ __________ a shower. (have)

4. He __________ (break) his leg __________ ____________________ his dog. (look for)

5. But not everything was bad:

______ he ______________ (lie) in hospital he __________ a beautiful nurse called Helen. (meet)

2. What does it mean?

1. Which of these sentences means 'Kevin started to put his tent up and then it rained'?

   ☐ When it started to rain Kevin *was putting* his tent up.
   ☐ When it started to rain Kevin *put* his tent up.

2. Which of these sentences means 'People didn't start to leave until Kevin arrived'?

   ☐ When Kevin arrived at the camp site everybody *was leaving.*
   ☐ When Kevin arrived at the camp site everybody *left.*

3. Which of these sentences means 'Kevin went to look for his dog. That's how he broke his leg'?

   ☐ When Kevin broke his leg he *looked* for his dog.
   ☐ When Kevin broke his leg he *was looking* for his dog.

3. How did it happen?

What happened to these people? Ask and answer the questions.

How did you break your leg, Kevin?

I *was looking* for my dog.

1. How ____________ Kevin ____________ sunburned? (get)

   He ____________ asleep while ____________ (fall – read)

2. What did Kevin do to his hand?

   He ________________________________ (burn – cook)

3. How ____ ?

   She ________________________________ a can of beans.

4. How ____ ? (fall)

   ____ (try to get)

4. What happened?

Write two sentences to describe these pictures.

2. a) When it started to rain we ____________ a picnic. (have)

   b) When it ________________________________

1. Wales and Germany

Megan's friend, Bernd, lives in Germany.
Megan comes from Wales. Sometimes they forget that Wales is an hour behind Germany.

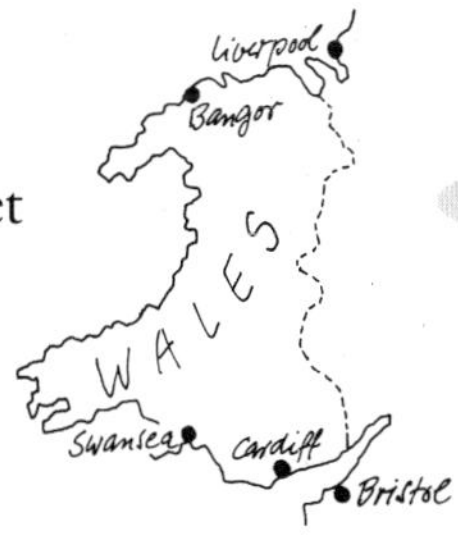

already – schon

Look what happened yesterday.

When Megan got up Bernd **had** already **finished** one lesson.

1. When Megan ______________ the morning's lessons Bernd ______________ ______________

2. At one o'clock Megan ______________ ______________ Bernd ______________ ______________ his homework.

3. At ______________ ______________ Bernd ______________ ______________ with his friends.

4. ______________ ______________ Bernd. But he ______________

When Megan *phoned* Bernd	he *had* already *gone* to bed.
this happened **later** *simple past*	this happened **first** *past perfect*

Für eine Handlung ______________________________ verwenden wir *simple past.*

Für eine Handlung ______________________________ jedoch *past perfect.*
Achte auf die Stellung von *already.*

2. A visit to Wales

Two years ago Bernd's older sister, Annette, visited Megan in Wales.
She loved it so much that she decided to stay.

By last August Annette *had* already *got* a job.

1. By last September she ________________________ a flat. (already – find)
2. By March she ________________________ Welsh. (already – learn)
3. By May she ____________________ in love with a Welshman. (fall)
4. And by June she ______________________ him. (marry)

3. She had not done it before

Before Annette went to Wales she *had* never *driven* on the left.

1. Before Annette _______ (go) to Wales she ________________________ Welsh. (hear)
2. Before ___________________ (visit) Megan she ___________________ darts. (play)
3. And she ____________________________ (drink) tea with milk before.

4. What about you?

Can you remember the first time you ever did something?

Before I	came to this school learned English went to lived met joined a … club	I **had** *never*	spoken English sung English songs played been to listened to made written	seen eaten used read had ridden

1. The desert – its people, its animals, its plants

Deserts are places where there is less than 100 millimetres of rain in one year.

People that live in deserts always have to look for water. Many are nomads who go from place to place. The Tuareg, for example, are nomads who live in the Sahara. They live in tents that they carry with them. They wear long clothes which keep the sun and sand out. Many desert people live in an oasis. An oasis is a place where there is water. Houses which are built in an oasis have small windows to keep the sun out.

Animals that live in the desert only come out in the mornings and evenings, when it's not too hot and not too cold. Some animals which live in deserts are camels, snakes and lizards.

Plants that grow in the desert must live for a long time without rain, like cacti. Sometimes we find fossils of trees which are millions of years old.

2. What can you say about deserts?

Put in *that, who* or *which.*

1. People that live in deserts …
2. Many are nomads …
3. The Tuareg live in tents …
4. They wear long clothes …
5. Animals … live in the desert …
6. Some animals … live in deserts are …

that, who, which, where = (in which)	
Für Menschen: ______________	Für Dinge und Tiere: ______________

3. Write a short article about deserts for a magazine

who *that*
which *where*

Use ideas like this:

Deserts are places *where* …

People *that/who* live in deserts …

Animals *that/which* live in deserts …

People
Nomads are people …
The Tuareg are people …
They live in tents/wear clothes …
An oasis is a place …
Houses that are built …

Animals
Some animals …
Camels are animals …

Plants
Plants … grow …
Sometimes – fossils of trees …

4. People you see in the desert

Look at these two sentences. Could you use *who* or *that* in the second sentence?

1. People *that* live in deserts are often nomads.
2. People you see in deserts are often nomads.

	People **who** live in deserts are often nomads. (Subjekt)
Das Relativpronomen im Nebensatz kann wegfallen, wenn es Objekt ist.	People (**who**) you see in deserts are often nomads. (Objekt)

Use relative pronouns (*who, which, that*) to finish these sentences.
If you don't really need the pronouns put them in brackets.

Example: People – live in deserts are often nomads.
People *who* live in deserts are often nomads.

1. Animals – live in the desert don't come out when it's hot.

___

2. Animals – you find in the desert don't come out – hot.

___

3. Some animals – we see in the deserts are camels, snakes and lizards.

___

4. Some animals – live in the deserts are …

___

5. Desert people wear long clothes – keep the sun out.

___

6. The clothes – desert people wear keep the sun out.

___

7. A cactus is a plant – doesn't need much water.

___

8. A cactus is a plant – you don't need to water much.

___

1. Where would you go?

1. *You:* Where would you go to see 'Dracula'?
   Your partner: ...

2. *Your partner:* Which number would you ring to call the police?
   You: ...

sell some old books
buy some jogging shoes
try some Indian food
call the operator
look for a flat
dance
have a cup of tea
get tickets for the concert
find a job

> Infinitiv mit **to**, um
> **Absichten** auszudrücken

2. Why did he go?

Yesterday Mike made a list of all the things he had to do.

- ring City Hall – order tickets
- post office – stamps
- Dawson's – new ping-pong balls
- book table Star of India
- take library books back
- ring bus station
  ask about buses to Sheffield
- bank – £30
- ring job centre
- Elsie's tea shop 4.30 – Maria

Why did he ring the City Hall?
To order tickets for the rock concert.

Why did he go to the post office? To ...
Why did he go to Dawson's?
Why did he ring the Indian restaurant?
Why did he go to the library?
Why did he ring the bus station?
Why did he go to the bank?
Why did he ring the job centre?
Why did he go to Elsie's tea shop?

1. Mrs O'Grady

Mrs O'Grady is talking to her grandson. She is telling him what life was like when she was a girl.
My parents made me help a lot at home. They made me do the washing and help with the shopping. They didn't let me go out with friends very much. Sunday was the best day. They didn't make me work on Sundays. In the afternoon they sometimes let me bring friends in. But they never let us have parties or play music.

Do you know what life was like for your grandparents or for other older people you know? Write down some questions to ask them.

Did your parents *make* you …?
Did your parents *let* you …?

Did your teachers *make* you …?
Did your teachers *let* you …?

help at home/with the …/ go to bed before …/stay in in the evenings/ be home by …/stay out/watch TV after …/ clean your teeth, wash … all the time/ go on holiday with friends/ go to …/ smoke/buy your own clothes/read/buy/ wear what you liked/leave school to get a job/ …

wear uniform/learn …/do homework every day/wear …/fight/eat in class/ chew chewing gum/stand up when the teacher came in/take radios to school/ sit where you liked/get there early/ …

make somebody do something – jemanden zwingen, etwas zu tun	**let** somebody do something – jemandem erlauben, etwas zu tun

2. And you?

Make four lists on a separate sheet of paper.

1. Things my parents/teachers make me do and they're right.
2. Things they make me do, but I don't think they're right.
3. Things they won't let me do and they're right.
4. Things they won't let me do, but I think they should.

Tell the class:

My … make me …
won't let

And (they're) right.
But I don't think …

1. What's the problem?

It's **too** wet **to** go out.

It isn't warm **enough to** go swimming.

It's **too** wet **to** go out. It isn't warm **enough to** go swimming.	**too** **enough** }	+ **Infinitiv**

(far, walk)

1. It's ______________________________

(have not enough change)

2. She ______________________________

(late, catch)

3. It's ________________________ a bus.

(heavy, carry)

4. Her bag is ________________________

(old, get in)

5. He isn't ______________________

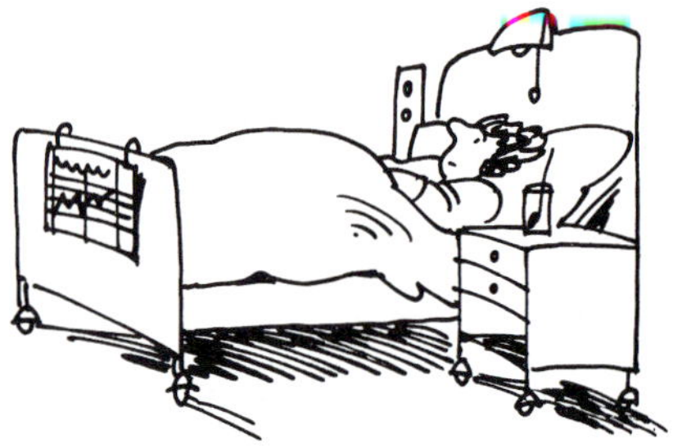

(ill, get up)

6. She is ______________________

(good, play in the team)

7. He is not ______________________

(dark, see)

8. It's ______________________ anything.

(money, buy sweater)

9. She hasn't ______________________

(dangerous, cross the road)

10. It's ______________________

(time, have lunch)

11. There's not ______________________

(difficult, eat)

12. Spaghetti is ______________________ !

1. Scott is fed up

She tells me	when what where who	+ to …

1. She tells me **when to go** to bed.
2. She tells me …
3. She tells me …

4. She …
5. She …
6. She …

2. Are you fed up?

Are you sometimes fed up because people tell you what to do?

They tell me … **to** …   **when to …**   **where to …**   **what to …**

how to …   **who to …**

3. Telling people what to do

Some people have to tell others what to do. It's their job.

The police tell you *what to do.*

Doctors tell you …… when you're ill.

People who write adverts tell you ……

Travel agents tell you …… for holidays.

Waiters tell you ……

Bus drivers tell you …… the bus.

Telephone operators tell you …… phone calls.

English teachers show you …… English.

Sports teachers …… games.

Music teachers …… instruments.

Cookery teachers …… cakes.

what – where – how (much) + **to**

buy – do – go – get off
learn – make – pay – play

4. I don't know what to do

When people visit foreign countries they don't always know what to do.
That's why they need phrase books. Phrase books tell them how to get help.

For example:

In the street

In the street

Can you tell me where to catch the bus to town, please?

I don't know how to use the phone. Could you help me, please?

In groups or with a partner think of some questions that should be in a phrase book for Germans visiting an English-speaking country.
Start your questions like this:

Can you tell me I don't know Could you show me	where how what	to …, please?

In the street
- get to the post office
- phone Germany
- find a chemist's
- stop a taxi

Travelling around
- get the bus to
- get off the (bus)
- get to
- buy a ticket
- change trains
- hire a bike
- fill in this form

At the bank
- change money
- cash a cheque
- do
- sign

Shopping
- find paper hankies
- get
- buy shoes

1. Thinking about energy

We need energy for for + …ing

– and for lots of other things. How many can you think of?

2. Saving energy

Most of the energy we use comes from coal, oil and gas.
If we use too much there soon won't be any left.
So what can we do about saving energy? This poster will give you some ideas.

SAVE ENERGY

- Collect and recycle.
- Buy recycled things.
- Don't buy things in packets and plastic bottles.
- Don't use plastic bags.
- Travel by bike, bus or train.
- Walk more.
- Have showers, not baths.
- Make birthday and Christmas cards. Don't buy them.
- Don't throw everything away without thinking.

Want to know more?
Write to us. We'll tell you how you can help.

Let's do something *about* saving energy.

We can help. For example by collecting and re ____________ things.

By ______________________ recycled things.

By not ____________________ ing things in ________________________

Can you go on?

1. How we learn things

Have you ever thought about how you learn things?
People have different ways of learning things. What is best for you?
Choose one or more of these ideas and finish the sentence like this or with words of your own:

helps me to learn (the language/remember them) – is better, more fun, easier – gives me the chance to say more

Example: *Explaining things to others helps me to learn.*

1. Listening to the teacher   Reading about things   Doing things
   Finding things out for myself   Explaining things to others
2. Working with a partner or in groups   Working alone
3. Doing homework with others   Doing homework alone
4. Saying things aloud   Writing things down
5. Reading English books and magazines   Talking to English people
   Listening to English radio, TV and songs   Going to English-speaking countries

2. What is school for?

These are some of the things that school helps us with.

Learning about the world   Working with a partner or in groups

Thinking about things

Can you think of any more things? Work with a partner or in groups and make a list. Start with words that end in *-ing: doing …, playing …, making …*

3. What is the most important?

Put the things on your list in order of importance – write 1 next to the most important, 2 next to the second most important and so on. If you can't decide you can give some things the same number, like this:

Doing sports	1
Having fun	1
Reading maps	2

Read out your list to the class:

I think …ing is the most important thing.

Can you say why the things on your list are important to you?

Reading/helps/teaches me to …/shows me how to …/is important because …

What do most people in your class find most important?

1. What sort of person are you?

	yes	no	sometimes
1. Do you enjoy being with other people?	☐	☐	☐
2. Do you like being alone?	☐	☐	☐
3. Would you prefer going to a party to watching TV at home?	☐	☐	☐
4. Do you enjoy being outside?	☐	☐	☐
5. Are you good at organising?	☐	☐	☐
6. Are you interested in learning new things?	☐	☐	☐
7. Are you afraid of doing something new?	☐	☐	☐

8. Write down two things you really love.
9. Write down two things you hate.
10. Write down two things you like doing, but never have time for.
11. How could you find more time?
    Stop ... (getting up late/talking on the phone/playing/going to/ ...).

(don't) like/hate/love/enjoy/prefer + ... ing
good at/interested in/afraid of + ... ing

I enjoy buying shoes.

I love lying in the sun.

I hate waiting for buses.

I hate sitting in a car for hours.

I like doing nothing.

2. What do you like doing?

Ask your partner:

- What do you want to be?
- ... because I like/enjoy .../ I'm good at/interested in ...
- What don't you want to be?

  ... because I don't like/hate .../ I'm not very good at/ interested in ...

pilot	computer programmer	talking to
architect	shop assistant	helping
baker	on a farm	travelling
cook	nature reserve	making things
secretary	office	cooking
designer	hotel	writing
bank manager	hospital	getting up early
journalist	working with animals/people	organising
hairdresser		learning languages
electrician		
engineer		

1. How?

What sort of a person is your partner?
How does he or she do these things? Put crosses in the boxes ☒.

1. How do you work at school – hard ☐, quite hard ☐ or not very hard ☐ ?
2. Can you usually do your homework easily ☐ or not so easily ☐ ?
3. Do you do your homework carefully ☐ or not so carefully ☐ ?
4. Do you think you speak English well ☐, not too badly ☐ or badly ☐ ?
5. How do you eat – quickly ☐ or slowly ☐ ?
6. How do you talk to your parents – always nicely ☐ or not always nicely ☐ ?
7. How do you normally talk – fast ☐, slowly ☐, loudly ☐ or quietly ☐ ?
8. How do you run – fast ☐ or not very fast ☐ ?
9. How do you walk – quickly ☐ or slowly ☐ ?
10. How do you read – fast ☐ or slowly ☐ ?
11. How do you ride your bike – carefully ☐, slowly ☐ or fast ☐ ?
12. How do you dance – beautifully ☐, quite well ☐ or badly ☐ ?
13. How do you like to dress – simply ☐, comfortably ☐, fashionably ☐ ?
14. How do you tell jokes – well ☐ or not too well ☐ ?

Underline all the adverbs in the questions you have just asked.

What kind of words do we make adverbs from?
Put the adverbs you have underlined into five lists to show the different ways they are made, e.g. *Adjectives that add …; Adjectives with … at the end; Adverbs that look like … etc.*

2. What is it like?

Finish the sentences with these words: *awful, beautiful, nice, wet, wonderful.*
Use each word once.

1. The grass is wet
2. The grass feels ____________________
3. The flowers smell ____________________
4. Your hair looks ____________________
5. The music sounds ____________________
6. This cheese tastes ____________________

Nach den Verben *be, feel, look, smell, sound, taste* verwenden wir ein ____________________

1. I'd like to be able to do it

What are they thinking? *(buy new clothes, dance, drive a car, play/sing like that, skate, use that, swim)*

1. I'd like to ......

2. ......

3. ......

4. ......

5. ......

6. ......

7. ......

8. ......

What about you?

I'd like **to be able** to ...

I'd like to **be able to** do that.
Für Fähigkeiten, die wir gern hätten.

2. What will or won't we be able to do?

Think of life a hundred years from now.
What will or won't people be able to do? What do you think?

People / They / Everybody	*will* *might*	*be able to …*
They	*won't* *might not*	*be able to …*

use computers
use machines for nearly everything
use the TV for shopping
buy newspapers, they'll be on TV
buy books, they'll be on cassettes
go shopping any time
live on other planets
go on trips to the moon
drive cars into towns

fly everywhere very cheaply
travel much faster
go out in the sun
swim in the sea
go skiing in the Alps
learn/work at home
speak two languages
use money, only cards
watch thousands of TV channels

1. If you saw these signs would you understand them?

You're **not allowed to** swim here.

1. You're ......

2. ......

3. ......

4. ......

5. ......

6. ......

7. ......

8. ......

am / is / are + *allowed to* – (dürfen)

2. At school

Write down three things you are *not allowed to* do at school.

1. We're not ________________________________

2. We're ________________________________

3. We ________________________________

Imagine you are the head teacher of a school. What are your school rules?

Pupils are/aren't *allowed to* …

3. At home

Imagine you have teenage children. What are and aren't they *allowed to* do?

They're *allowed to* …

They're not / They aren't *allowed to* …

1. What might happen?

It **might** rain.

1. ......

2. ......

3. ......

4. ......

5. ......

6. ......

7. ......

might (not) –
vielleicht (nicht)

2. What about you?

This afternoon Tonight Tomorrow At the weekend
Next year When I leave school In twenty years' time

I **might** ...

I **might not** ...

Charlie always forgets things, but he's very lucky. Look what happened in the last few weeks. Lots of other things **might have** or **could have** happened but, thank goodness, they didn't.

> Something **might/could have** happened
> It was possible, but it didn't happen.

One day he *dropped* his camera.
It *might/could have broken,* but it didn't.

The next day he … the … without looking (cross). He … an accident (have), but he didn't.

The day after that he … his … (fall off). He … something (break), but he …

On … he … some old … (eat).
He … ill (be), but he wasn't.

… he … some tablets on the table (leave). His sister … them (eat), but …

… he … to meet his aunt at the station (forget).
She … very angry (be), but …

… he … to deliver the newspapers (forget).
He … his job (lose), but …

… he … his jacket on the bus (leave).
He … it (lose), but …

… he … some money on his desk (leave).
Someone … it (take), but they …

… he … the budgie's cage open (leave).
It … away (fly), but …

… he … his glasses on a chair (put).
Someone … on them (sit), but they …

… he … a monkey at the zoo (feed).
It … him (bite), but …

1. What does this house tell you?

The Wilsons are moving into this house.
What does the house tell you about the people who lived here before?

They/Someone **must have** … They **can't have** …

2. Jokes

Can you finish these jokes? Put in *must be* or *must have.*

1. Johnny has been playing the piano for four years.

   – Has he? His fingers ____________________ tired!

2. *Hairdresser:* Were you wearing a red scarf when you came in?
   Customer: No. Why?

   Hairdresser: Oh, then I ____________________ cut you.

3. *Man:* Is this a good river for fish?

   Fisherman: Well, they don't want to come out, so it ____________________ .

4. *Customer:* This café ____________________ a very clean kitchen.
   Waiter: Thank you. But how do you know?
   Customer: Because everything tastes of soap.

1. An African family

Miriam is thirteen. Her family lives in Africa. They have some land, but not much money. Her father and brother, Nelson, work hard in the fields so that they can all have enough to eat. Nelson is ten. Miriam's mother makes all their clothes. When Miriam gets up she goes and washes in the river. It is about one kilometres away from her home. She carries water back home on her head. Then she makes a fire and helps her mother to make breakfast. After breakfast she walks three kilometre to the market to sell fruit. She carries it in a basket on her head. In the afternoon Miriam and her mother go to the river to wash the clothes. When it is dark they go to bed. They all live and sleep in one room on the floor. They are all very tired.

Our life isn't as hard, is it?
We don't need to do lots of these things.

Compare life in your country with Miriam's family.

> We **don't need to/needn't** work so hard.
> She **doesn't need to** (brauchen nicht)

My father/mother/sister/brother *doesn't need to/needn't …*
We/Children *don't need to/needn't …*

2. A hundred years ago

Now think of your own country a hundred years ago.
There are lots of things that people didn't need to do.

People/They/Children *didn't need to …*

travel far to work
learn to …/so many things
remember know
wait on motorways for hours
go everywhere by car
stay at school for so long
do so much homework/so many tests
take so many exams
learn other languages
know about computers
use so much electricity/energy
look at their watches all the time
get so much information
think of the environment …

3. And the future?

What will or won't people need to do a hundred years from now?

They *will/won't need to …*

go to school
learn at home/computers
build schools
write on paper
buy newspapers
post letters
clean/cook
go shopping
go to work
five days a week

1. Thinking about young people

Read out these ideas to your partner. Put crosses (x) to show what he or she thinks. Then your partner asks you.

	yes	no	don't know
1. There should be more places for young people to go.	☐	☐	☐
2. Young people should stay at school as long as they can.	☐	☐	☐
3. Pupils should wear uniforms.	☐	☐	☐
4. Boys and girls shouldn't be in mixed classes.	☐	☐	☐
5. Girls should be allowed to play football;	☐	☐	☐
boys should learn cooking and sewing.	☐	☐	☐
6. There shouldn't be any homework.	☐	☐	☐
7. School shouldn't be free.	☐	☐	☐
8. The summer holidays shouldn't be so long.	☐	☐	☐
9. There shouldn't be so many tests.	☐	☐	☐
10. Young people should leave home after 18.	☐	☐	☐
11. All families should spend some time together every day.	☐	☐	☐
12. Young people should be able to go out without telling their parents where they are going.	☐	☐	☐
13. Young people should get money for doing jobs at home.	☐	☐	☐
14. Young men shouldn't have to go into the army.	☐	☐	☐
15. Young women should go into the army.	☐	☐	☐
16. Young people should visit as many different countries as they can.	☐	☐	☐
17. There are some jobs that women shouldn't do.	☐	☐	☐
18. Young people shouldn't get married before they have jobs.	☐	☐	☐
19. Women should have children when they are young.	☐	☐	☐
20. Young people should help other people more.	☐	☐	☐
21. Most young people are only interested in earning a lot of money.	☐	☐	☐

2. My ideas

Now write down your ideas about young people.

– Young people *should/shouldn't* …

3. What I would like

Everybody has a different idea about the ideal boyfriend or girlfriend. What about you?

– My boy/girlfriend *should/shouldn't* (be/like/have/ …)

And what sort of a place would you like to live in?

It There	*should/shouldn't*	be	(near/hot/have/ …)

What a holiday!

These people are all on holiday. But they are not enjoying it very much.
So many things have gone wrong. Why? What *should* or *shouldn't* they have done?

They **shouldn't have** gone by car.

Sally's bag didn't arrive.
She **should have** put her address on it.

1. bring so many clothes

2. change his money

3. check when … are open

4. be in the sun for so long

5. walk about in the rain

6. buy a map

7. go swimming there

8. eat so much

9. learn the language

10. leave … open

11. leave

12. water

13. tell the postman about their …

14. leave things … fridge

1. Where would you like to go?

You can speak English quite well, now.
Which English-speaking country would you like to go to?
What would you do there?
Write down your ideas and tell the class:

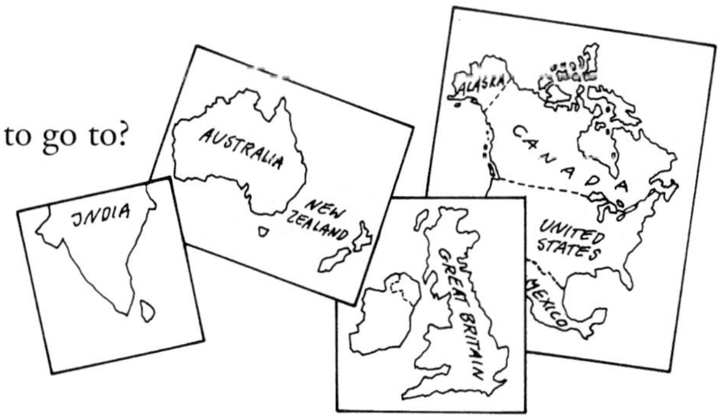

I'd like ______________________________

I'd ______________________________

____

____

2. Ask your classmates and write their answers down

Where would you like to go?
What would you do there?

Country	What I would do
America	*go and see Hollywood, visit ...*

3. Tell me

Make some cards like this. You can write four of your own ideas.
Ask your classmates.

Where would you like to go?	France Italy America Turkey

What would you like to do this weekend?	Go swimming Play tennis ______ ______

What would you like to be?	A pop singer A film star A teacher ______

Which pop star would you like to meet?	______ ______ ______ ______

1. What teenagers want

The teenagers in this survey talked about what they wanted or would like in life. They also said what they didn't want or wouldn't like.

want – wollen
would like – möchten

	I want	I'd like	I don't want	I wouldn't like
a career	18 %	12 %	40 %	30 %
lots of money	42 %	28 %	12 %	18 %
to have children	15 %	25 %	38 %	22 %
to travel	50 %	30 %	12 %	8 %
to work outdoors	20 %	16 %	34 %	30 %

Can you explain this table?

– Eighteen per cent want a career. Twelve per cent would like a career.
– Forty per cent …

2. What about you and your classmates?

– Tell me: What do you want and what don't you want in life?

I (really) want …
I don't want …
I'd hate …
I'd (quite) like …
I wouldn't like …

lots of fun, interesting job, live, have, learn, work in, with, go and see, get married, be a …

Vorsicht:

I want – ich will
I will – ich werde

Tell the class about you and your partner:

I (don't) want …
(Axel) wants/doesn't want …
… would(n't) like …

3. Make a class survey

I want	I'd like	I don't want	I wouldn't like

…% want …
…% don't want …
…% would like …
…% wouldn't like …

1. Signs and advertisements

What do the people who wrote these signs and advertisements want us to do? What don't they want us to do?

They **want** people to drive slowly.

They **don't want** us to feed the animals.

2. They want me to …

It's not only advertisers that want us to do things, is it?
Other people often want us to do things, too.

Our teachers *want us to …*
They *don't want us to …*

My … *wants me to …*
She *doesn't want me to …*

stay out	go to
buy	go out with
wear	have
watch	help
eat	get up
learn	do homework

3. I want them to …

Sometimes you want other people to do things, don't you?

I want my brother to stop taking my things.

I don't want my friend to go to parties without me.

I *want … to …* / I *don't want …* to …

give	take	wear
lend	let	stop criticising
help	talk about	
show	use	

4. Your children?

If you had children what would you want them to do?
What wouldn't you want them to do?

I'd **want them to …** I **wouldn't want them to …**

How young people in different parts of the world live

Clothes
In hot countries people wear clothes that are long and made of thin material. The sari, for example, is worn by Indian women.

Some people wear special clothes to show that they are in an organisation. In some schools, for example, uniforms are worn.

School
Not all young people can go to school. In some parts of Australia many children live hundreds of kilometres from the nearest school. Lessons are sent to them by post and they are taught by teachers over the radio. In hot countries children are often taught outside. In India some children are taken to school by rickshaw. Others walk or go by bus.

Transport
In many countries buses are the most popular form of transport. Luggage is carried on top of them. They are often decorated with pictures and flowers.

Food
Most Chinese and Asian meals are made of rice. This is mixed with meat or vegetables and a sauce. Chinese food is mostly vegetables that are cooked very quickly in a pan. The pan is called a wok. Woks are used for cooking nearly everything in China. The food is eaten with two sticks, called chopsticks. In Italy many people eat pasta every day. It is made of flour, water and oil.

Birthdays
People all over the world celebrate birthdays, but not in the same way. In China one year is added to everyone's age at the Chinese New Year, which is between 21 January and 19 February. Birthdays are only celebrated at the age of ten, and then every ten years after that. In Switzerland a tree is planted when a baby is born, a pear tree for a girl and apple for a boy. On Mexican birthdays a ball is made out of papier mâché. It is called a piñata. It is filled with small presents. When the birthday party is over the children break it and take the presents out.

Passiv ohne *by* …
Children **are taught** outside.

Wir **wissen nicht** oder halten für **unwichtig, wer** etwas tut.

Passiv mit *by* …
Children **are taught** *by* teachers over the radio.

Die **Handelnden** werden besonders **betont.**

1. Wildlife in danger

All around the world many wonderful animals, birds and plants are disappearing[1] from the earth. It is thought that one type of animal, bird or plant is lost every half hour.

Some are being killed because they are beautiful. People want to wear them, to make shoes out of them or to decorate their floors and walls with them. Gorillas' hands and feet are being sold as souvenirs.

Millions of birds are being taken from South American forests and put into cages as pets. Butterflies are being collected by unthinking people. Forest plants (e.g. orchids) are being taken and sold as house plants. Some animals and birds are even being killed for 'sport'.

The biggest problem is that the homes of animals, birds and plants are being destroyed[2] all the time. Rain forests, for example, are being cut down. The wood is being sold and exported, mostly to Europe. The land is being used by farmers, to produce more meat for things like hamburgers. Every hour 24 sq km of rain forest disappear. Homes are being taken away from the people who live there. They are having to go to the towns.

Wildlife is also disappearing because of the changes that are being made to the land. More and more roads, shops, houses and car parks are being built. Wild, natural land is being made into farmland. Wetlands are being dried and filled in for farming and building. Many places that used to be quiet are now being visited by tourists. And so the wildlife that lived there is being destroyed. Many animals, birds and plants are also being killed by chemicals in the rivers, the land and the atmosphere.

[1] to disappear – verschwinden

[2] to destroy – vernichten

Land **is being used** for farming.

Butterflies **are being collected** ***by*** unthinking people.
Many animals **are being killed** ***by*** chemicals.

Passiv ohne ***by:*** Wir **können** oder **wollen** die Handelnden **nicht** genau **bestimmen.**

Passiv mit ***by:*** Wer oder was etwas **verursacht**, wird besonders **betont.**

2. Informing other people

Other people might not know as much as you do about the problems with wildlife.
Make a poster so that more people will understand.

Wildlife in danger!

Did you know that all the time many wonderful animals,

birds and plants ______________________________ ?

Some ____________________ because they are beautiful.

Birds ________________ from ________________

They ____________________ into cages as pets.

Butterflies ______________________________

Plants ______________________________

Animals and birds ______________________________

Rain forests ______________________________

The wood ______________________________

The land ______________________________

Wildlife is also disappearing because more and more roads, ________

____

Wild, natural land ______________________________

And so the wildlife that lived there ____________________

Many animals, birds and plants ____________________

____

3. What can be done?

Think of some ways in which we can stop wildlife from disappearing.

We *shouldn't* …
We *could* …
We *should* stop people from …

buy	for (decoration)
stop buying	build too many
furs	put so many
skins	chemicals
wood	join an organisation
take from	

1. How much do you know?

Did you know?

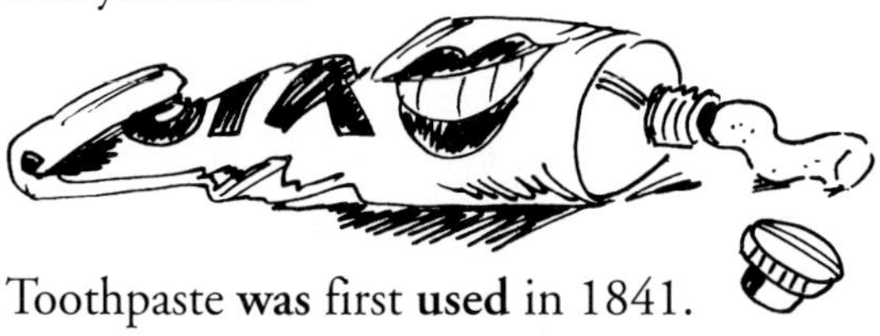

Toothpaste **was** first **used** in 1841.

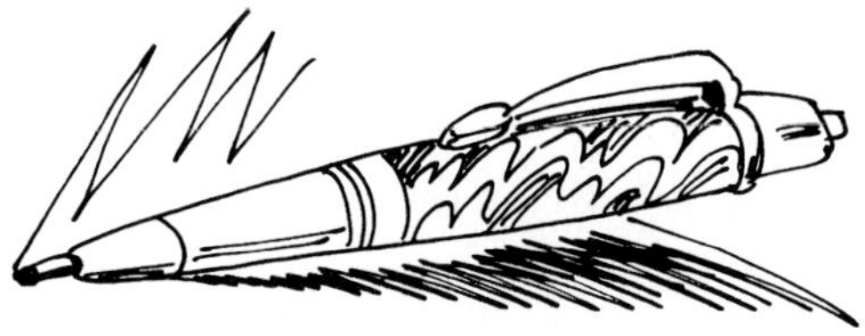

The first biros **were made** *by* a Hungarian.

Passiv ohne ***by:***	**Passiv mit** ***by:***
Toothpaste **was** first **used** in 1841.	The first biros **were made** *by* a Hungarian.
Wir **wissen nicht** oder halten für **unwichtig, wer** etwas tat.	Der **Handelnde** wird besonders betont.

1. The earliest numbers ________________ about 5,000 years ago. (write)
2. The first alphabet ________________ in Syria about 3,500 years ago. (use)
3. The first Christmas card ________________ in 1853. (send)
4. Paper ________ first ________________ by the Chinese in 105 AD. (produce)
5. The first biros ________________ Lazlo Biro from Hungary. (make)
6. Pencils ________________ in the 1790s in France and England. (first, make)
7. Felt-tips ________________ the Japanese in 1964. (first, use)
8. Personal computers ________________ in the 1970s. (first, sell)
9. Plastic ________________ in 1862. (first, produce)
10. The ________ watch ________________ a Bavarian in 1504. (first, make)
11. The ________ bar of chocolate ________________ in 1819. (first, make)
12. Tobacco ________________ the American Indians. (first, smoke).
    It ________________ to Europa in the 1500s. (bring)
13. Movies ________________ in New York in 1885. (first, see)

2. A quiz

Make two teams. Four people from each team go to the front as a panel.
Someone from team A gives the four at the front from team B some information.
Sometimes it is correct, sometimes it is wrong.

The first alphabet was used 3,500 years ago. Is that right or wrong?

Pencils were first made in the nineteen hundreds.

Felt-tips were first used by Germans.

1. Headlines

How good is your English? Can you understand these headlines?

£ 2 MILLION SPENT ON NEW SPORTS CENTRE	FILM STAR KILLED IN ACCIDENT

Two million pounds **have been spent** on a new sports centre.

A film star …

300 toys collected by pupils for children's home	**Baby found in woods by dog**

300 toys …

A baby …

A film star **has been killed.**	A baby **has been found** *by* a dog.
Passiv ohne *by:* **Wer** oder **was** eine Handlung **verursacht** hat, ist **unwichtig.**	**Passiv mit** *by:* Der **Verursacher** wird **betont.**

2. Explain in more detail what these headlines tell us

Write sentences like this: … **has/have been** … *(by)* …

GIRL GIVEN MEDAL FOR SAVING CHILD

Two baby gorillas born in zoo

Bestseller written by schoolboy

TWO-THIRDS OF RAIN FORESTS CUT DOWN IN 3 YEARS

FILM MADE BY SCHOOLCHILDREN

City centre closed to cars

World chess record broken by computer

Youth club opened in old factory

Trip round world won by 15-year-old

RACE WON BY OXFORD

Paintings stolen by cleaner

SIX TAKEN TO HOSPITAL AFTER TRAIN CRASH

1. Life in a hundred years' time

People have lots of ideas about what life will be like
in a hundred years' time.
Which of these ideas do you think will be true for your country?
Put a cross (x) under R for *right* or W for *wrong*.

	R	W
At school		
1. Children won't be taught by teachers, but by machines.	☐	☐
2. Children won't be taught in schools, but at home.	☐	☐
3. Every pupil will be given a computer.	☐	☐
4. Pupils will be tested by computers.	☐	☐
5. Pupils will be sent to different countries to learn the languages.	☐	☐
6. English will be taught to all seven-year-olds.	☐	☐
At work		
7. Much more work will be done at home.	☐	☐
8. More jobs will be shared.	☐	☐
9. People won't be allowed to work more than two days a week, so that everyone will have a job.	☐	☐
10. Much more work will be done by robots.	☐	☐
11. All big buildings will be cleaned by robots.	☐	☐
12. Post won't be sent by the post office any more, but by fax machines.	☐	☐
At home		
13. Robots won't be used in private homes.	☐	☐
14. Everything will be cooked in microwave ovens.	☐	☐
15. Not so much meat will be eaten.	☐	☐
16. Not many people will be married.	☐	☐
17. Not so many babies will be born.	☐	☐
In towns		
18. People won't be allowed to take their cars into towns.	☐	☐
19. Electricity will be used for all cars.	☐	☐
20. New cities will be built.	☐	☐
21. Films won't be shown at cinemas any more. They will only be watched at home.	☐	☐
22. More shopping will be done by phone.	☐	☐
23. Everything will be paid for by plastic cards.	☐	☐
Other changes		
24. Buildings won't be heated by oil, but by solar energy.	☐	☐
25. The wind will be used much more for energy.	☐	☐
26. Newspapers won't be sold in shops any more, they will be read on TV.	☐	☐
27. Sports won't be played outside because of the ozone.	☐	☐
28. Sometimes people will be told not to go outside because of the ozone.	☐	☐

English **will** still **be spoken** in most countries. Children **won't be taught** *by* teachers.	**will** **won't**	+ **be** + **past participle**

2. Write down some of your ideas about the future

… will/won't/might/might not …

1. A word puzzle

1. It **should be kept** in a fridge.
2. This **doesn't have to be kept** in a fridge.
3. It **can be eaten** with the fingers.
4. This **can't be eaten** with the fingers.

B	U	T	T	E	R				
			B						

	Hilfsverb +	be +	past participle
It	has to should/shouldn't	be	eaten with the fingers.

2. Now you make up the clues

Use: *can('t) – has/have to – must(n't) – should(n't) + passive.*

1. It … every day. (eat)
2. It … in bottles or cartons. (sell)
3. It … in a bottle. (buy)
4. In Britain it … at the chemist's. (buy)
5. They … to children. (sell)
6. They … at British post offices. (buy)
7. They … in Britain. (use)
8. It … in some British schools. (wear)
9. They … of plastic or wood. (make)
10. It … on your desk. (leave)
11. They … by bike riders. (wear)
12. They … on motorways. (ride)
13. They … onto planes. (take)
14. They … into Britain. (take)
15. They … on a walking holiday. (take)
16. They … for walks every day. (take)
17. It … outside or inside. (play)
18. It … by two teams. (play)

F	R	U	I	T					
M	I	L	K						
B	R	E	A	D					
A	S	P	I	R	I	N			
C	I	G	A	R	E	T	T	E	S
P	O	S	T	C	A	R	D	S	
P	O	U	N	D	S				
U	N	I	F	O	R	M			
D	E	S	K	S					
M	O	N	E	Y					
H	E	L	M	E	T	S			
B	I	K	E	S					
K	N	I	V	E	S				
A	N	I	M	A	L	S			
M	A	P	S						
D	O	G	S						
F	O	O	T	B	A	L	L		
B	A	S	K	E	T	B	A	L	L

1. Is it worth it?

The alarm clock rings. Seven o'clock. "What, already?" thinks Steve. Ten minutes later he closes the door behind him and starts to run down the road.

Sometimes he wonders if it is really worth it. But then he imagines how great it would be to win a medal for Britain. His girlfriend is beginning to complain that she never sees him. But then, on a day like this, with the sun shining and the birds singing, he really enjoys himself running through the fields.

An hour later he is back home. He washes and dresses for school, then sits down to a breakfast of bacon and eggs. He has to hurry and cuts himself with a knife. Yesterday he burned himself on the toaster. At half past eight he leaves the house. "Bye, love," his mother says, "look after yourself". "I will. See you later," he answers. He has to hurry to catch the bus to school.

At a quarter past four Steve gets on the bus again and goes home. By now he is feeling very tired, so he lies down for half an hour before tea. Later, when he has done his homework, he relaxes, makes himself a cup of cocoa and listens to music. Then he starts to feel very tired. He falls asleep. He imagines he has won an Olympic medal ...

2. What do they say?

Use *cut, burn, enjoy* (2), *look after,* and *make* (2) with the correct reflexive pronouns.

Reflexive Pronouns			
I	myself	we	ourselves
you	yourself	you	yourselves
he	himself	they	themselves
she	herself		

1. Steve has ____________ a training plan. In the week he trains for an hour every day and two hours at the weekend.
2. In the mornings, when her children have gone to school, Steve's mother ____________ a cup of tea and reads the newspaper.
3. Steve's mother worries a lot about her children. They tell her, "Don't worry, Mum. We can ____________".
4. Steve is telling his friend what happened yesterday – "I ____________ on the toaster".
5. Steve's little sister is cutting bread. Steve warns her, "Don't ____________"
6. Steve and his friend are invited to a party. His mother says, "Bye. ____________"

3. Translate into English

First try to do it without looking at the text.

1. Steve fragt sich oft, ob es sich wirklich lohnt.
2. Seine Freundin beklagt sich, dass er so oft weg ist.
3. Morgens muss sich Steve beeilen.
4. Kurz nach acht wäscht er sich und zieht sich für die Schule an.
5. Nach der Schule fühlt sich Steve oft sehr müde.
6. Manchmal legt er sich für eine halbe Stunde hin.
7. Abends entspannt er sich.
8. Er hört sich oft Musik an.
9. Er stellt sich manchmal vor, er habe bei der Olympiade eine Medaille gewonnen.

Underline the reflexive verbs in the German sentences and the English verbs you used to translate them.

4. Fill in this table with verbs from text 1 and your translations

English verbs – not reflexive	German verbs – reflexive
__________	__________
__________	__________
__________	__________
__________	__________
__________	__________
__________	__________
__________	__________
__________	__________

1. Simon Cox, 20 years

I get along quite well, really. Washing and dressing is no problem. And I can make my own breakfast. I can't get out of bed myself, though. I need help for that. And I can't wash my hair myself. My girlfriend helps me. But I can do the washing, the ironing and the cooking. I can't make my bed myself and I can't clean the flat myself either. Mrs Bailey from next door helps me. I help her, and her husband, too. You see, it's difficult for them to do their shopping themselves because Mr Bailey can't walk very far. Now I've got a car, but I can't get into it myself. I can drive it, though. So we all do the shopping together.

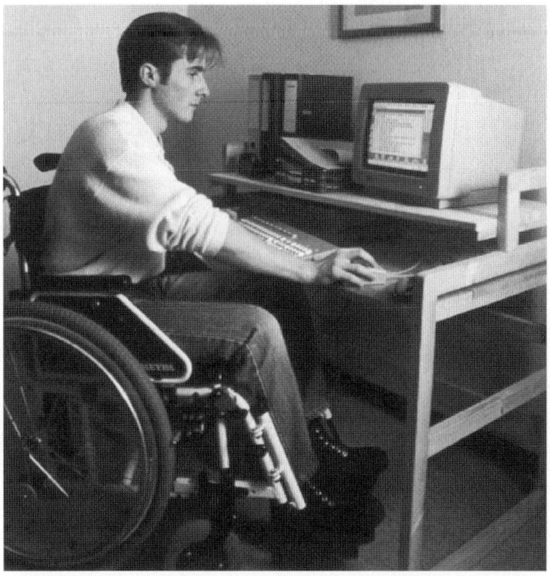

He can do it him**self**. They can't shop them**selves**.	Sind die Reflexivpronomen auf der zweiten Silbe **betont**, bedeuten sie „**selbst**".

Have you got a good memory?

Someone asks you about Simon and his neighbours. How much can you remember about them? Cover the text up and use sentences like this:
– He can't make his bed **himself**.
– The Baileys … **themselves**.
– He can/can't … **himself**.

2. What problems do they have?

1. wash and comb her hair

2. get out of bed

3. do the cooking

4. do the washing

5. carry his bag

6. get down

7. stand up

8. open the door

3. Old people

City School wants to start a project to help the old people
who live near them.
One class is going to talk to old people who live alone – single people.
Another class wants to talk to couples – two people living together.
What questions could they ask?

Single people	*Couples*
Can you ... **yourself**?	Can you ... **yourselves**?

get out of bed do the washing/ironing/ ...?

4. Can you help?

Is there anyone you know who might need help?
What can't they do themselves? How could you help?

Man in post office: Shall I stick the stamp on myself?
Assistant: No. Put it on the envelope.

1. Ann shows Mark her town

Ann's friend Mark has come to see her. They are standing on a bridge over the town and Ann is telling Mark what all the buildings are.

Ann explains:
The hospital is behind the supermarket, the chemist's and a department store.
The chemist's is between the supermarket and the department store.
The supermarket is the long building.
The police station is next to the railway station. Opposite the police station is the cinema.
There's a café on the corner. The one with the balcony. In summer you can sit outside in the garden. One of the buildings behind the park is a sports centre.
The tall building next to it is a block of flats. In front of the park is the library.
On the right of the library is a restaurant and next to the restaurant is a hotel, the one with the cars in front of it. The post office is next to the cinema. And there's a bank opposite the library.
On the right of the bank is our job centre.

2. Which one is it?

Ask your partner two questions like this. Then your partner asks you.
Then you ask another two – and so on.

Which building is the post office?	**The one** next to/in front of …
And **which one** is the …?	**The** big **one** with the …

Which one is the bank? *The one* on the corner.	Mit **one** vermeiden wir Wiederholungen.

Write the names of the buildings on them.

3. How much do you know about the world?

Einzahl
Which one?

Mehrzahl
Which ones?

Its cities?

1. Which of these cities are in Europe?
   Singapore – Milan – Delhi – Vienna?
2. Which ones are in Britain?
   Brussels – Nottingham – Belfast – Washington
3. Which ones are in Scotland?
   Glasgow – Newcastle – Hull – Edinburgh
4. Which ones are in Wales?
   Bristol – Cardiff – Liverpool – Bangor

Its countries?

1. Which of these countries are in Europe?
   Japan – Portugal – Peru – Greece
2. Which ones have mountains?
   Switzerland – Holland – Nepal – Belgium
3. Which ones are hot?
   Greenland – Spain – Alaska – Australia
4. Which ones are next to the sea?
   Ireland – Hungary – Austria – Bulgaria

A 1

If I: Realer Bedingungssatz

Thema dieser Einheit sind Vor- und Nachteile des Massentourismus, den grammatischen Schwerpunkt bildet der „reale Bedingungssatz". Als Einstieg bietet sich ein allgemeines Gespräch über den Massentourismus an, wobei der Wortschatz dieser Einheit schon vorweggenommen werden kann, z. B.:

L: *Where do you go on holiday? What kind of places do you like? What about places where there are lots of big concrete hotels on the beach/by the sea?* (evtl. Tafelskizze oder mitgebrachtes Bild).
But some countries need tourism, don't they? Look at this place, for example, (zeigt Bild auf Arbeitsblatt, evtl. auf Folie).
Places like this need money to build schools and hospitals. And they don't get enough from fishing. How do you think places like this will change if they get lots of tourists? What will the people have to do? (Mögliche Antworten: *Build hotels, shops, restaurants, car parks, swimming pools, cinemas).*
What else will happen? (There will be more cars. They'll need more land for building, so there won't be enough land for the villagers. And it will be too expensive. The villagers will have to live somewhere else; There will be more jobs, but the young people might not want to go fishing any more/do the old jobs. People might get new ideas from the tourists. There might be problems/conflicts with the old way of life).

Tourism – yes or no?
Nach der allgemeinen Einführung wird der Eingangstext gelesen (vom Lehrer, von Schülern oder in Stillarbeit). Danach wird eines der Argumente für den Tourismus als Beispiel für einen realen Bedingungssatz herausgegriffen: *If tourists come we'll be able to build a better school.* Bevor sich die Schüler mit der anschließenden Übung beschäftigen, wird die Struktur ***If + simple present + future*** durch einen Merkkasten in Erinnerung gerufen.
Die Übung, in der die Lernenden durch Lückensätze und Stichworte angedeutete verschiedene Meinungen ausformulieren, ist für Gruppen- oder Partnerarbeit gedacht.
Im ersten Teil der Übung – *Arguments for tourism* – werden Argumente für den Tourismus formuliert.

● Lösungen
2. *If we don't get more money we won't have enough schools.*
3. *If more people come I'll sell more things.*
4. *If tourists come I'll get a job in a hotel.*
5. *If tourists don't come I'll have to close my café.*

Im zweiten Teil der Übung folgen Argumente gegen den Tourismus. Die Schüler arbeiten in Gruppen oder mit einem Partner.

● Lösungen
1. *If tourists come they will need hotels, shops and restaurants.*
2. *If we build hotels, shops and car parks there won't be enough land for us.*
3. *If more people need land it will get more expensive.*
4. *If the land is too expensive we won't be able to live here.*

● Lösungen *(Can you go on?)*
If tourists come they will use a lot of water.
If there are more tourists there will be more cars.
If there are more cars the air will be dirtier.
If tourists don't come the village will stay clean and quiet.
If we have a tourist industry the young people will not go fishing any more.

Weiterführendes Gespräch
Die Schüler machen sich Gedanken darüber, wie das besprochene Dorf Touristen anlocken könnte, ohne den Lebensstil der Bevölkerung zu zerstören, z. B.:

L: *These people need more money and tourism would help. Can they have tourism without spoiling too much?*

● Mögliche Vorschläge
The tourists could stay in people's houses. They could build small hotels and not too many. They could only allow a few/limited numbers of tourists to come.
They could talk to the tourists about their problems/take the tourists to the schools and hospitals/show the tourists the village and ask them to help. They could start an exchange programme ...

A 2

If II: Irrealer Bedingungssatz

Irreale Bedingungssätze werden anhand des fächerübergreifenden und die Lebenswirklichkeit der Schüler direkt tangierenden Themas der Umweltproblematik geübt.

1. The world we live in
Die beiden auf dem Arbeitsblatt erscheinenden Bilder können zunächst ohne Text auf dem OHP gezeigt werden. Ohne die zu übende Struktur zu erwähnen, werden Schülerbeiträge gesammelt, wobei der für den weiteren Verlauf der Einheit nützliche Wortschatz eingeführt wird, z. B.:

L: (Zeigt das linke Bild) *What kind of problems does this picture show? Can you talk about them in English?*
S1: *There are a lot of cars/'s a lot of traffic.*
S2: *The air's very dirty.* usw.
L: *This is a big problem in towns and cities, isn't it? What could we do about it? Any ideas?*
S1: *People could go by train.*
S2: *We could use buses more often.* usw.

Das rechte Bild wird gezeigt:

L: *Now look at this picture. Would you like to live next to this rubbish (dump)? No, of course you wouldn't. We collect so much rubbish, but no-one wants to live near it. So what could we do?*
S1: *We could recycle more.*
S2: *We could stop buying plastic bottles/things in packets/ ...* usw.

In einem nächsten Schritt werden die zu den Bildern gehörenden Sätze gezeigt *(If there weren't ...; If we recycled ...).*

What do you think?
In Gruppen- oder Partnerarbeit schreiben die Lernenden anschließend einige Vorschläge zur Vermeidung von Umweltverschmutzung auf, wobei sie die beiden angegebenen Strukturen und den vorgeschlagenen Wortschatz benutzen. Sie sollten außerdem dazu ermutigt werden, nach unbekanntem Wortschatz zu fragen bzw. zu suchen.

● Mögliche Vorschläge
If – we/people used buses/trams/trains/bikes (more often)
If – two people had/used/drove one car/shared a car
If – we/people had/used/drove electric or solar cars the air would be cleaner.
We wouldn't have so much rubbish if
– we/people didn't buy things in packets/plastic bottles/cans;
– people used things more than once (like plastic bags);
– people used baskets or bags, not plastic ones, for shopping;
– we collected things and used them again/recycled them.
Die Ideen werden nun der Klasse vorgetragen. Anschließend wird anhand der beiden Beispielsätze auf dem Arbeitsblatt die Regel erklärt. Je nach Klasse kann man die im Merkkästchen erscheinende Regel von den Schülern aus den Beispielsätzen ableiten lassen.

2. How could we make the world a better place?
Der sich mit der Verbesserung der Umwelt beschäftigende Gedankengang wird weitergeführt.

● Lösungen
1. *If we used bikes and buses more often there would not be so many cars.*
2. *If there were not so many cars the air would be cleaner.*
3. *If we did not put so many chemicals into the sea the water would be cleaner.*
4. *It would be better for the land, too, if we did not use so many chemicals.*

Any more ideas?
Anschließend können die Schüler mithilfe der angegebenen Strukturen ihre Gedanken etwas freier formulieren. Diese Übung eignet sich besonders für Gruppenarbeit, z.B.:
We could save energy if we used the sun and the wind (more).
We could save water if we had showers, not baths.

A 3

Past continuous

Um das *past continuous* wieder in Erinnerung zu rufen, schaut der Lehrer auf seine Uhr und berichtet:
L: *Yesterday at this time I was (teaching .../doing/marking/ ...) What about you?*
Als Hilfestellung für die Antworten können einige Vokabeln angegeben werden, z. B. *learning English/doing maths, sports, a test/writing/playing.*

1. What were they all doing?
Die Zeitangaben *between (four) and (six)* und *from (six) to (eight)* können eingeführt werden durch die Aufforderung an die Schüler, zu erzählen, was sie am vorigen Tag während einer bestimmten Zeitspanne taten. Gleichzeitig kann die folgende erste Übung des Arbeitsblattes wortschatzmäßig vorentlastet werden:
L: *What were you doing yesterday between four and six in the afternoon? – Taking the dog for a walk? Having a party? Jogging?*
S1: *I was ...ing.*
S2: *I was ...*
usw.
Anschließend wird die Übung auf dem Arbeitsblatt mündlich und/oder schriftlich, im Klassenverband, in Einzel- oder Partnerarbeit gemacht.

● Lösungen
I was learning to use a computer.
I was having a drink with a friend.

What did Andy and Liz say?
Between four and six we were washing the car.
From six to about seven we were taking the dog for a walk.
Between seven and twelve we were dancing at a party.

And Johnny?
Between four and six I was painting the bathroom.
From six to seven I was watching (a film on) TV.
Between eight and twelve I was playing (the guitar) in a band.

And what about Donna and Tony?
From five to six we were jogging.
Between six and eight we were watching a football match.
Who was not telling the truth? – Donna und Tony: das Fußballspiel hat erst um 20.00 angefangen.

2. What were you doing?
Die Klasse fertigt Karten für ein Kettengespräch an (vgl. Arbeitsblatt). Die linke Seite besteht aus Gesprächseröffnung und Frage, die rechte aus einer Antwort. Die Lücken werden individuell ergänzt. Schüler 1 eröffnet das Gespräch und richtet seine Frage an Schüler 2. Schüler 2 antwortet und eröffnet das Gespräch mit Schüler 3 usw.

A 4

Past continuous und simple past

Um eine möglichst flexible Verwendung des Kontrastpaares *past continuous* und *simple past* zu fördern, werden diese Zeitformen in verschiedene syntaktische Strukturen eingebettet:
While he was putting his tent up it rained.
(Übung 1)
Someone stole his radio while he was swimming.
(Übung 1)
How did you break your leg? – I was looking for my dog.
(Übung 3)

1. Kevin's holiday
Um das Thema eines misslungenen Campingurlaubs einzuführen, kann der Lehrer über ein ähnliches, fiktiven Bekannten zugestoßenes Missgeschick erzählen. Dabei wird eventuell unbekannter Wortschatz der ersten Übung schon vorweggenommen:
L: *I met some friends last night. They were telling me about their holiday. It was terrible. They wanted to go by car. But while they were putting everything into their car their dog ran away. So they went to look for it. But while they were looking for the dog their little boy fell down and broke his finger. When they finally left it was nearly midnight. And then – they were driving down the motorway when suddenly the car stopped. They had no petrol left. So they decided it would be better to just stay at home.*

Das erste Bild auf dem Arbeitsblatt – ohne den dazugehörigen Text – wird auf den OHP gelegt:
Look, here's someone else who had a terrible holiday, too. This is Kevin. Look what happened to him. While he was putting his tent up …
S1: *It rained.*
L: *Yes.* (Bild 2): *But he finally managed to put it up. Then he went for a swim. But then – look what happened: Someone stole …?*
S2: *His radio.*
L: *That's right. Someone stole his radio while he was swimming.*

Im Anschluss an das Einführungsgespräch werden die ersten beiden Sätze des Arbeitsblattes aufgedeckt, wobei der zweite Satz zu vervollständigen ist. Dann wird, wie auf dem Arbeitsblatt angedeutet, die Regel für die Kontrastierung von *past continuous* und *simple past* zusammen mit den Lernenden erarbeitet.

● Lösungen
Someone stole his radio while he was swimming.
Für eine Handlung in der Vergangenheit, die unterbrochen wurde, verwenden wir *past continuous.*
Für die neu einsetzende Handlung *simple past.*

Sätze 1–5 werden nun mündlich und/oder schriftlich im Klassenverband, in Einzel- oder Partnerarbeit vervollständigt.

● Lösungen
1. *He fell asleep while he was reading and got sunburned.*
2. *While he was cooking he burned/burnt his hand.*
3. *His dog ran away while he was having a shower.*
4. *He broke his leg while he was looking for his dog.*
5. *While he was lying in hospital he met a beautiful nurse called Helen.*

2. What does it mean?
Um ihr Verständnis der unterschiedlichen Funktionen von *past continuous* und *simple past* nachzuweisen, sollen die Schüler aus Satzpaaren jeweils den Satz aussuchen, der einer vorgegebenen Aussage am nächsten kommt.

● Lösungen
1. Satz 1 2. Satz 2 3. Satz 2

3. How did it happen?
In dieser Übung werden Fragen im *simple past* mit Aussagen im *past continuous* kontrastiert:
How did you break your leg, Kevin? – I was looking for my dog.

● Lösungen
1. *How did Kevin get sunburned?*
He fell asleep while he was reading.
2. *He burned/burnt it while he was cooking.*
3. *How did she cut her finger?*
She was opening/trying to open a can of beans.
(Bemerkung: Im britischen Englisch setzt sich analog zum amerikanischen Englisch *can* anstelle von *tin* immer mehr durch.)
4. *How did the man/he fall into the water?*
He was trying to get his hat.

4. What happened?
Zur Festigung der unterschiedlichen Bedeutungen von *past continuous* und *simple past* wird ein Bildpaar beschrieben, das die Schüler zu einer differenzierenden Verwendung dieser Zeitformen herausfordert.

● Lösungen
1. a) *When it started to rain we were having a picnic.*
b) *When it started to rain we had a picnic.*

A 5

Past perfect

In dieser Einheit wird das *past perfect* in folgenden Satzkonstellationen geübt:
1. *When Megan got up Bernd had already finished one lesson.* (Übung 1)
2. *At nine o'clock Megan phoned Bernd. But he had already gone to bed.* (Übung 1)
3. *By last August Annette had already got a job.* (Übung 2)
4. *Before Annette went to Wales she had never driven on the left.* (Übungen 3 und 4)

1. Wales and Germany
Das Thema *Wales* kann mittels eines kurzen, allgemeinen Gesprächs, unterstützt durch eine Landkarte von Großbritannien, eingeleitet werden, z. B.:
L: *I'm sure you've heard of a country called Wales. Can you find it on this map? What do you know about Wales?*
Nach einigen Schülerbeiträgen liest der Lehrer den Einführungstext von Übung 1 vor. Die Übung wird in Partnerarbeit durchgeführt.

● Lösungen
1. *When Megan finished the morning's lessons Bernd had already gone home.*
2. *At one o'clock Megan had lunch. Bernd had already started his homework.*
3. *At six o'clock Megan started her homework. Bernd had already gone out with his friends.*
4. *At nine o'clock Megan phoned Bernd. But he had already gone to bed.*

Wie im Merkkästchen angedeutet, kann die Regel für die Anwendung des *past perfect* zusammen mit den Schülern erarbeitet werden:
Für eine Handlung in der Vergangenheit verwenden wir *simple past.*
Für eine Handlung davor jedoch *past perfect.*

Anschließend können die Schüler einige Vor- und Nachteile des englisch-walisischen und deutschen Schulsystems diskutieren (z. B. samstags kein Unterricht in England und Wales, dafür aber jeden Nachmittag; Schuluniform oder nicht etc.).

2. A visit to Wales
In der Satzkonstellation dieser Übung ist das *past perfect* als abhängige Zeit schwieriger zu erkennen, da der das *simple past* enthaltende Nebensatz fehlt und durch die Zeitangabe *by (last August)* ersetzt wird. Das Zeitverhältnis lässt sich durch eine syntaktische Erweiterung der Zeitangabe verdeutlichen: *By the time last August arrived …*

Die Übungssätze werden zuerst mündlich und dann schriftlich vervollständigt. Dabei sollte auf die verkürzte Aussprache von *had,* z. B. [ʃi:d] für *She had,* geachtet werden.

● Lösungen
1. *By last September she had already found a flat.*
2. *By March she had already learned Welsh.*
3. *By May she had fallen in love with a Welshman.*
4. *And by June she had married him.*

3. She had not done it before
● Lösungen
1. *Before Annette went to Wales she had never heard Welsh.*
2. *Before Annette visited Megan she had never played darts.*
3. *And she had never drunk tea with milk before.*

4. What about you?
Nach den vorausgegangenen stark gelenkten Übungen sollen die Lernenden das *past perfect* nun etwas freier anwenden, indem sie über eigene Erfahrungen schreiben und sprechen. In Einzel- oder Partnerarbeit schreiben sie mit Hilfe der angegebenen Strukturen und Vokabeln drei bis fünf Sätze über sich selbst, z. B.:
Before I came to this school I had never played volleyball.
Before I learned English I had never sung English songs.
Before I went to Switzerland I had never seen a mountain.
Before I went to England I had never had tea with milk.
Anschließend lesen einige Schüler ihre Sätze vor.

A 6

Notwendige Relativsätze mit und ohne Pronomen: that, who, which, where

Die ersten drei Übungen befassen sich mit Relativpronomen in notwendigen Relativsätzen. In der vierten Übung wird verdeutlicht, dass die Relativpronomen dann weggelassen werden können, wenn sie sich auf das Objekt des Nebensatzes beziehen *(contact clauses).*

1. The desert – its people, its animals, its plants
Der Eingangstext kann durch ein allgemeines Gespräch über Wüsten, am besten durch eine Weltkarte unterstützt, vorbereitet werden. An dieser Stelle lassen sich auch schon die im Text vorkommenden unbekannten Wörter einführen, z. B.:
L: *Are any of you good at geography? Can you tell me what a desert is?* (Nach Schülerbeiträgen): *A desert's a place where there's not much water and so not much can grow* (evtl. Tafelskizze). *Do you know the names of any deserts?* Schülerbeiträge: *Sahara, Gobi, Death Valley, Mohawe, Thar* usw.
L: *What else do you know about deserts?*
Der Text kann noch weiter vorentlastet werden, indem man das Gespräch in Abschnitte, die dem Textaufbau entsprechen, einteilt: Menschen in der Wüste (Nomaden, Suche nach Wasser, Kleidung, Oasen); Wüstenflora und -fauna.
Nach einigen Schülerbeiträgen wird der Text gelesen (Lehrervortrag oder stilles Lesen).

2. What can you say about deserts?
Die Übungssätze werden schriftlich, in Einzel-, Partner- oder Gruppenarbeit vervollständigt und dann vorgelesen. Dabei sollen die Schüler ermutigt werden, eigene Ideen einzubringen und nach unbekanntem Wortschatz zu suchen bzw. zu fragen.

● Lösungen
1. *People that live in deserts always have hot weather/always have to look for water/have to live near water/wear long clothes because of the sun and the sand/often ride camels/ …*
2. *Many are nomads who don't live in one place/move from place to place.*
3. *The Tuareg live in tents that they carry with them.*
4. *They wear long clothes which keep the sun and sand out.*
5. *Animals that live in the desert only come out in the mornings and evenings.*
6. *Some animals which live in deserts are camels, snakes and lizards.*

Die Regel im Merkkästchen kann von den Schülern anhand der vorausgegangenen Beispielsätze erarbeitet werden:
Für Menschen: *that, who*
Für Dinge und Tiere: *that, which*

3. Write a short article about deserts for a magazine
In Partner- oder Gruppenarbeit und unter Anwendung der vorgegebenen Strukturen und Informationen schreiben die Schüler einen Artikel über die Wüste.

4. People you see in the desert
Ein Relativsatz, bei dem ein Pronomen verwendet werden muss, wird mit einem inhaltsgleichen Relativsatz kontrastiert, bei dem das Pronomen weggelassen werden kann. Derartige Vergleiche erleichtern das Verständnis der beiden unterschiedlichen Strukturen. Die Regel für den Wegfall des Relativpronomens beschränkt sich auf dessen Funktion als direktes Objekt *(contact clause).*
Die Sätze können im Klassenverband, in Einzel- oder in Partnerarbeit vervollständigt werden. Je nach Leistungsstand, kann man versuchen, die Regel zusammen mit den Lernenden zu erarbeiten.

● Lösungen
- In Satz 2 könnte *who* oder *that* erscheinen:
  2. *People who/that you see in deserts are often nomads.*
  (*Whom* wird nur noch selten gebraucht).
- In Satz 1 bezieht sich das Relativpronomen auf das Subjekt, in Satz 2 auf das Objekt.

1. *Animals that/which live in the desert don't come out when it's hot.*
2. *Animals (that/which) you find in the desert don't come out when it's hot.*
3. *Some animals (that/which) we see in the deserts are camels, snakes and lizards.*
4. *Some animals that/which live in the deserts are camels, snakes and lizards.*
5. *Desert people wear long clothes that/which keep the sun out.*
6. *The clothes (that/which) desert people wear keep the sun out.*
7. *A cactus is a plant that/which doesn't need much water.*

8. *A cactus is a plant (that/which) you don't need to water much.*

Weiterführendes Projekt
Die Lernenden können aufgefordert werden, weitere wissenswerte Informationen über Wüsten zusammenzutragen.

A 7

Infinitiv mit to: Absicht

1. Where would you go?
Zur Einstimmung fordert der Lehrer die Lernenden auf, sich vorzustellen, sie seien in einem englischsprachigen Land und würden die auf dem Arbeitsblatt abgebildeten Annoncen lesen:

L: *You can all speak English quite well now – well enough to visit a country where they speak English. Let's say/imagine you're in Britain and you see all these adverts. Let's see if you can understand them all.*
Where would you go, for example, to see the film "Dracula"?

S1: *To the City Cinema.* (Die Schüler sollten nicht gezwungen werden, unnatürlich ausformulierte Sätze zu produzieren wie etwa *I would go to the City Cinema).*

L: *Yes, that's right. You'd go to the City Cinema to see "Dracula", wouldn't you?*
And let's say you see an accident. Which number would you ring to call the police?
usw.

Die folgenden zwei Fragestrukturen werden an die Tafel geschrieben:
Where would you go to …?
Which number would you ring to …?
Es kann schon zu diesem Zeitpunkt auf die Funktion des Infinitivs in dieser Einheit hingewiesen werden, nämlich „Absichten ausdrücken".
In Partnerarbeit stellen sich zwei Schüler abwechselnd jeweils eine Frage zu den Annoncen, wie auf dem Arbeitsblatt vorgeschlagen. Um zu gewährleisten, dass jeder Partner beide Fragestrukturen übt, sollten die Fragen in der Reihenfolge der Wortvorgaben auf dem Arbeitsblatt gestellt werden:

1. *You: Where would you go to see "Dracula"?*
   Your Partner: To the City Cinema.
2. *Your Partner: Which number would you ring to call the police?*
   You: 999.
3. *You: Which number would you ring to sell some old books?*
   Your Partner: 443009.
4. *Your Partner: Where would you go to buy some jogging shoes?*
   You: Dawson's.
   usw.

● Lösungen
Bei den Telefonnummern wird 0 wie „o" ausgesprochen [əʊ]; Doppelzahlen *"double three"* usw.).
Which number would you ring to sell some old books? – 443009.
Where would you go to buy some jogging shoes? – Dawson's.
Where would you go to try some Indian food? – The Star of India.
Which number would you ring to call the operator? – O.
Which number would you ring to look for a flat? – 634198.
Where would you go to dance? – The Dreamland Disco.
Where would you go to have a cup of tea? – Elsie's tea shop.
Which number would you ring to get tickets for the concert? – 769425.
Which number would you ring to find a job? – 237501.

2. Why did he go?
Die abgedruckten Fragen können entweder im Klassenverband oder in Partnerarbeit gestellt und beantwortet werden, wobei die Antworten lediglich – und ganz natürlich – aus Infinitivkonstruktionen bestehen, z. B. *To order tickets for the rock concert.*
Variante: Ein Gedächtnisspiel, bei dem sich die Lernenden in einem ersten Schritt Mikes Merkzettel einprägen und in einem nächsten Schritt vom Lehrer mithilfe der abgedruckten Fragen befragt werden. Die Antworten werden mündlich und/oder schriftlich gegeben.

● Lösungen
Why did he go to the post office? – To buy/get some stamps.
Why did he go to Dawson's? – To buy/get some new ping-pong balls.
Why did he ring the Indian restaurant? – To book a table.
Why did he go to the library? – To take his (library) books back.
Why did he ring the bus station? – To ask about buses to Sheffield.
Why did he go to the bank? – To get thirty pounds.
Why did he ring the job centre? – To ask about a job.
Why did he go to Elsie's tea shop? – To meet/see/have tea with/Maria.

A 8

Infinitiv ohne to: make, let

Die Strukturen *make/let s.o. do sth.* können durch ein allgemeines Gespräch über Ge- und Verbote für Jugendliche eingeführt werden, wie etwa:

L: *You know, I'm glad I'm not a young person like you any more. So many people tell you what to do and what not to do, don't they? There are teachers and parents. They make you do this and they won't let you do that.*
Teachers, for example – they make you learn all sorts of things. They make you do tests. They won't let you play music. They won't let you run around. What else do they make you do? What won't they let you do?

Als Hilfestellung werden die beiden verwendeten Strukturen an die Tafel bzw. auf den OHP geschrieben:
They make you …
They won't let you …
Nach einigen Schülerbeiträgen wird die erste Übung eingeführt.

1. Mrs O'Grady
Das Bild von Mrs O'Grady kann zunächst ohne den dazugehörigen Lesetext auf dem OHP erscheinen, wobei der Text zur Übung des *listening comprehension* vorgelesen wird. Alternativ lesen die Schüler den Text laut oder still.

Do you know what life was like for your grandparents …?
Mithilfe des angegebenen Wortschatzes schreiben die Schüler in Gruppen- oder Partnerarbeit einige Fragen auf, die sie älteren Verwandten oder Bekannten stellen könnten, z. B.:

Did you parents make you …?
- *help at home/with the washing/shopping/ …*
- *go to bed before …*
- *stay in in the evenings*
- *be home by …*
- *clean your teeth, wash your hands all the time*
- *leave school to get a job*

Did your parents let you …?
- *stay out after …*
- *watch TV after …*
- *go on holiday with friends*
- *go to discos/all night parties …*
- *smoke*
- *buy your own clothes*
- *read/buy/wear what you liked/ …*

Did your teachers make you …?
- *wear uniform*
- *learn (English)*
- *do homework every day*
- *stand up when the teacher came in*
- *get there early*

Did your teachers let you …?
- *wear jeans/trainers/what you liked*
- *fight*
- *eat in class*
- *chew chewing gum*
- *take radios to school*
- *sit where you liked*

Als Hausaufgabe können die Schüler ältere Menschen aus ihrem Bekannten- und Verwandtenkreis befragen und in der nächsten Englischstunde unter Verwendung der zu übenden Strukturen darüber berichten, wie etwa:

S1: *I asked my grandfather/uncle/neighbour.*
His parents/teachers made him …
They let him …
They didn't make/let him …

2. And you?
In Einzel-, Partner- oder Gruppenarbeit stellen die Lernenden stichwortartig vier Listen zusammen, z. B.:
1. *clean my teeth, work hard*

Anschließend berichten sie der Klasse unter Verwendung der angegebenen Strukturen:
My … make(s) me … And he's/she's/they're right.
My … won't let … /But I don't think (he's) right/ he should.

A 9

Infinitiv mit to: too, enough

1. What's the problem?
Zur Einstimmung schaut der Lehrer aus dem Fenster und macht Bemerkungen wie *What's the weather like today? I think it's too cold/wet to go out/warm enough to go swimming outside/not warm enough to sunbathe.*

Danach werden die Bilder auf dem Arbeitsblatt unter Anwendung der angegebenen Strukturen im Klassenverband oder in Partnerarbeit mündlich und/oder schriftlich beschrieben.

● Lösungen
1. *It's too far to walk.*
2. *She hasn't enough change to make a phone call/for a phone call.*
3. *It's too late to catch a bus.*
4. *Her bag is too heavy to carry.*
5. *He isn't old enough to get in.*
6. *She is too ill to get up.*
7. *He is not good enough to play in the team.*
8. *It's too dark to see anything.*
9. *She hasn't enough money to buy the sweater.*
10. *It's too dangerous to cross the road here.*
11. *There's not enough time to have lunch.*
12. *Spaghetti is too difficult to eat!*

A 10

Infinitiv mit Fragewörtern: where/when/how to …

1. Scott is fed up
Das Thema der ersten Übung sowie der Ausdruck *fed up* können eingeführt werden durch das Aufzählen von ärgerlichen Situationen, z. B.:

L: *You know, sometimes I get really fed up, don't you? I get fed up when I have to mark homework for hours. And I get fed up when I have to say the same things again and again. I get fed up, too, when I don't have time for my hobbies.*
What about you? (Als Hilfestellung wird *I get fed up when …* an die Tafel geschrieben).
S1: *I get fed up when …* usw.

Nach einigen Schülerbeiträgen lesen die Lernenden die erste Übung in Stillarbeit und beschreiben die Bilder mündlich und/oder schriftlich.

● Lösungen
2. *She tells me when to get up.*
3. *She tells me what to wear.*
4. *She tells me what to eat.*
5. *She tells me where to go.*
6. *She tells me who to go out with.*

Zur weiteren Übung decken die Schüler die Bilder zu und berichten aus dem Gedächtnis und in der 3. Person Singular über Scott:
Scott's sister tells him when to get up. She (also) tells him what to wear usw.

2. Are you fed up?
Das Gespräch wird auf Situationen gelenkt, in denen sich die Lernenden bevormundet fühlen. In Gruppen- oder Partnerarbeit und unter Verwendung des angegebenen Wortschatzes stellen die Schüler eine Liste derartiger Situationen zusammen, z. B.:

They tell me – *when to go to bed/eat/tidy my room/do my homework/ …*
– *what to wear/read/watch on TV/do in my free time/ …*

– *where to go in the evenings/with my friends/ …*
– *how to dress/have my hair/ …*
– *who to go out with/bring home/ …*

3. Telling people what to do
Mündlich und/oder schriftlich, im Klassenverband, in Partner- oder Einzelarbeit werden die Sätze in Übung 3 vervollständigt.

● Lösungen
Doctors tell you what to do when you're ill.
People who write adverts tell you what to buy.
Travel agents tell you where to go for holidays.
Waiters tell you how much to pay.
Bus drivers tell you where to get off the bus.
Telephone operators tell you how to make phone calls.
English teachers show you how to learn English.
Sports teachers teach/show/tell you how to play games.
Music teachers teach/show/tell you how to play instruments.
Cookery teachers teach/show/tell you how to make cakes.

Fortgeschrittenere Schüler können versuchen, weitere ähnliche Sätze selber zu formulieren, z. B.:
Geography teachers teach/show/tell you how to read/draw maps.
Biology teachers teach/show you how to understand plants and animals.
Chemistry teachers teach/show you how to do experiments.
usw.

4. I don't know what to do
Zur Einführung in das Thema „Sprachführer für Touristen" beginnt der Lehrer ein Gespräch über Verständigungsschwierigkeiten von Touristen im Ausland:
L: *Sometimes you really need people to tell you what to do, for example when you're in a foreign country. Let's say you're in Britain on holiday. You're in a town and you want to catch a bus to the town centre. But you don't know where the bus stop is. What would you say?*
S: *Can you tell me where the bus stop is for town, please?*
L: *Yes, or you could say, "Can you tell me where to catch the bus to town, please?"* (Die unterstrichenen Wörter werden an die Tafel bzw. auf Folie geschrieben).
You might have other problems, too, like finding the station or buying bus tickets or using the phone. There are little books that help you in situations like that. They're called phrase books. Let's find out a bit more about them. Look at exercise four.
Nach dem einführenden Gespräch wird die Übung in Gruppen- oder Partnerarbeit zuerst schriftlich gemacht und dann mündlich vorgetragen. Die Schüler sollten ermutigt werden, die angegebenen Wortschatzvorschläge zu variieren und nach unbekannten Wörtern zu suchen bzw. zu fragen.

● Mögliche Vorschläge
Can you tell/show me …
I don't know …

In the street
– *how to get to the (post office)/phone Germany/stop a taxi*
– *where to find a (chemist's)*

Travelling around
where to catch/get the bus to … /get off the bus (for the town hall)/buy a ticket/change trains (for Sheffield)
– *how to get to (Nottingham)/hire a bike/fill in this form*

At the bank
– *how to change money/cash a cheque*
– *what to do*
– *where to sign*

Shopping
– *where to find (paper hankies)/get …*
– *where to buy shoes*

A 11

-ing-Form nach Präpositionen: for, by, about

1. Thinking about energy
Als Einstieg dient ein allgemeines Gespräch über Energie, z. B. über den Energieverbrauch im Klassenzimmer. Gleichzeitig wird der Wortschatz eingeführt, der für die nachfolgende Übung notwendig ist:
L: *Have you ever thought how much energy we use? Here, for example, here in this classroom? We need energy for lighting and* (deutet auf die Heizung und das Waschbecken) …?
S1: *Heating.*
S2: *Washing.*
L: *Yes, we need energy for heating and for washing.* (Die unterstrichenen Wörter können aufgeschrieben werden).
Now look at this picture (Arbeitsblatt). *What else do we need energy for?*
Die Vorschläge können im Klassenverband, in Einzel- oder Partnerarbeit, mündlich und/oder schriftlich gemacht werden. Die Lernenden sollten ermutigt werden, nach unbekanntem Wortschatz zu suchen bzw. zu fragen.

● Lösungen
(We need energy) for washing – for travelling/going/coming to school – for cooking – for keeping food cool – for making and filling packets/making … – for lighting – for heating – for watching TV/using computers/playing computer games/using video recorders/playing games with batteries/using things with batteries/ …

2. Saving energy
Mithilfe des auf dem Poster angegebenen Wortschatzes sammeln die Schüler Ideen, wie man Energie einsparen könnte.

● Lösungen
We can help by collecting and recycling things.
By buying recycled things.
By not buying things in packets and plastic bottles.
By not using plastic bags.
By travelling by bike, bus or train.
By walking more.
By having showers, not baths.
By making birthday and Christmas cards (and not buying them).
By not throwing everything away without thinking.

Weiterführendes Projekt
Die Schüler können ermutigt werden, an Organisationen zu schreiben, die sich mit dem Energieproblem beschäftigen, z. B. Greenpeace, Friends of the Earth.
Greenpeace UK, Canonbury Villas, London N1 2PN, England.
Friends of the Earth, 26/28 Underwood St., London N1 7JQ, England.

A 12

-ing-Form als Subjekt

1. How we learn things
Als Einstieg dient ein kurzes Gespräch über das Lernverhalten verschiedener Schüler in der Klasse. Gleichzeitig wird unbekannter Wortschatz zur Entlastung der folgenden Übung eingeführt, z. B.:

L: *You have to learn lots of things in school, don't you? Have you ever thought about how you learn? You see, some people say that listening to the teachers is best. Others think that reading about things helps them more. Others say that finding things out for themselves is the best way.*
(Die unterstrichenen Ausdrücke werden aufgeschrieben).
What about you? What's best for you?
S1: *Reading about things.*
S2: *Finding things out for myself.*
usw.

Die erste Übung wird in Einzelarbeit gemacht.
Außer den angegebenen Antwortvorschlägen können die Schüler auch eigene Ideen einbringen. Bei den Punkten 1 und 5 lassen sich gleichzeitig mehrere Aussagen machen, z. B.:

1. *Finding things out for myself helps me to learn/is better/more fun.*
Listening to the teacher is easier/boring.
Doing things in groups is more fun.
Explaining things to others helps me to learn.
usw.

2. What is school for?
Die Lernenden machen sich Gedanken und sprechen darüber, was sie in der Schule alles lernen. In Partner- oder Gruppenarbeit erstellen sie Listen ihrer Vorschläge, z. B.:
Reading
Writing
Learning different languages
Learning how to do things
Learning to get on with all sorts of different people
Helping others to learn
Making friends
Making things with my hands
Learning things so I can get a job
Playing musical instruments
Passing exams
Having fun
Anschließend lesen ausgewählte Paare/Gruppen ihre Listen vor.

3. What is the most important?
In Partner- oder Gruppenarbeit erstellen die Lernenden eine Prioritätenliste. Sollten sie sich nicht klar entscheiden können, dürfen sie die Vorschläge auch in Prioritätengruppen ordnen, wie auf dem Arbeitsblatt vorgeschlagen.
Anschließend berichten einzelne Schüler über ihre Ergebnisse. Sie sollten ermutigt werden, weitere Erklärungen zu geben, z. B.:

S1: *Working in groups is the most important thing to me. It helps me to learn.*
S2: *I think reading and writing are the most important, because if you can't read or write you can't get a job.*
usw.

Es kann auch ein Klassenspiegel erstellt werden. Eine Strichliste zeigt, was den meisten Lernenden am wichtigsten ist und dokumentiert die Prioritäten der Gesamtklasse.

A 13

-ing-Form als Objekt, nach Adjektiven und Präpositionen und nach stop

Das Hauptgewicht dieser Einheit liegt auf der *-ing*-Form als Objekt nach bestimmten Verben *(enjoy, like, prefer, love, hate)*, es wird jedoch auch die *-ing*-Form nach *good at, interested in, afraid of* und *stop* geübt.

1. What sort of person are you?
In Partnerarbeit stellen sich jeweils zwei Schüler die auf dem Fragebogen abgedruckten Fragen. Zuerst stellt Partner A alle Fragen, dann Partner B. Anschließed referieren einzelne Schüler über ausgewählte Antworten ihrer Partner, z. B.:

L: (Thomas), *how did your partner answer questions one to three?*
S1: (Martin) *enjoys being with other people. But sometimes he likes being alone. He prefers going to a party to watching TV at home.*
usw.

2. What do you like doing?
Analog dem abgebildeten Mustergespräch und mithilfe der angegebenen Redemittel befragen sich die Schüler gegenseitig über ihre Vorlieben und Abneigungen in Hinsicht auf Berufe und Arbeitsstätten. Die Gespräche können entweder im Klassenverband oder in Partner- bzw. Gruppenarbeit erfolgen.

A 14

Adverbien der Art und Weise

1. How?
Die Adverbien der Art und Weise werden mittels eines Fragebogens geübt. Als Einstieg erscheinen die Abbildungen zweier Jugendlichen an der Tafel bzw. auf dem OHP (Strichzeichnungen oder ausgeschnittene Bilder). Unter Anwendung von Adverbien der Art und Weise werden die Jugendlichen miteinander verglichen, z. B.

L: *Look at these two friends (sisters, brothers). They're very different from each other. Jenny* (L. deutet auf eine der Figuren) *works very hard at school.* (Die Adverbien können aufgeschrieben werden). *She always works carefully. And she never has problems with her homework. She always does it quickly and easily.*

Now her friend, Simon, doesn't work hard at all. He doesn't work carefully. He always does everything too fast and very carelessly. He has a lot of problems with his homework. He can never do it easily, like Jenny. He often has to ask her for help.

Nach dieser Einführung spricht der Lehrer einzelne Schüler an. Dabei können die unbekannten Wörter des nachfolgenden Fragebogens eingeführt werden, z. B.:

L: *What about you* (S1)*? Do you work hard at school? Quite hard or not very hard?* (Alternativfrage zwingt die Schüler, die Adverbien selbst zu verwenden).
S1: ...
L: *And you* (S2)*? Do you work carefully or not so carefully?* usw.

In einem zweiten Schritt werden die Lernenden dazu aufgefordert, den Fragebogen mit einem Partner durchzuarbeiten. Zuerst stellt Partner A alle Fragen und kreuzt die Antworten an, dann werden die Fragen von Partner B gestellt. Anschließend können einzelne Schüler der ganzen Klasse über ihre Partner berichten, z. B.: (Manfred) *works hard at school. He usually does his homework easily. He doesn't always do it carefully.* usw.

Underline all the adverbs in the questions you have just asked.
Die folgenden Adverbien werden unterstrichen: *hard, easily, carefully, well, badly, quickly, slowly, nicely, fast, loudly, quietly, beautifully, simply, comfortably, fashionably.*

What kind of words do we make adverbs from? Adjectives

Put the adverbs you have underlined into five lists to show the different ways they are made.
In Gruppenarbeit versuchen die Lernenden, die unterstrichenen Adverbien in fünf Kategorien einzuteilen. Je nach Klasse können die Kategorien vorgegeben werden.

● Lösungen
1. *Adjectives that add -ly: carefully, badly, quickly, slowly, nicely, loudly, quietly, beautifully*
2. *Adjectives with y at the end (y becomes i): easily*
3. *Adjectives with -le at the end (changes to ly): simply, comfortably, fashionably*
4. *Adverbs that look like adjectives: hard, fast*
5. *Irregular adverbs: well*

Die Schüler können aufgefordert werden, zusätzliche, ihnen bekannte Adverbien in die Listen einzutragen.

2. What is it like?
In dieser Übung wiederholen die Schüler, dass nach bestimmten Verben *(be, feel, smell, look, sound, taste)* kein Adverb, sondern unerwarteterweise ein Adjektiv steht. Die Lückensätze werden mit den angegebenen Adjektiven vervollständigt, wobei darauf zu achten ist, dass jedes Wort mit Ausnahme von *wet* nur einmal verwendet werden darf und vom Sinn her zutreffend sein muss.

● Lösungen
2. *The grass feels awful/beautiful/nice/wet/wonderful.*
3. *The flowers smell awful/beautiful/nice/wonderful.*
4. *Your hair looks awful/beautiful/nice/wet/wonderful.*
5. *The music sounds awful/beautiful/nice/wonderful.*
6. *This cheese tastes awful/beautiful/nice/wonderful.*

Die Regel kann zusammen mit den Schülern erarbeitet werden:
Nach den Verben be, feel, look, smell, sound, taste verwenden wir Adjektive.

Weitere Übung (nicht auf dem Arbeitsblatt)
Eine weitere Lernschwierigkeit bereitet die Stellung des Adverbs der Art und Weise im Satz, wenn auf das Verb ein Objekt folgt. Während im Deutschen die Modifizierung des Verbs zwischen Verb und Objekt stehen kann, stehen im Englischen die Adverbien der Art und Weise nie zwischen Verb und Objekt. Diese verschiedene Satzstellungen lassen sich am besten durch eine Übersetzungsübung verdeutlichen, z. B.:
1. Susanne spricht gut englisch. *Susanne speaks English well.*
2. Lothar öffnete langsam den Brief. *Lothar opened the letter slowly.*
3. Karin machte schnell das Fenster zu. *Karin closed the window quickly.* (Aus stilistischen Gründen erscheint das Adverb manchmal vor dem Verb – *Karin quickly closed the window).*

Nach der Übersetzungsübung kann die Regel zusammen mit den Schülern erarbeitet werden.

A 15

Be able to

1. I'd like to be able to do it
Als Einstieg zeigt der Lehrer Bilder, die verschiedene Fähigkeiten darstellen, z. B. Ausüben verschiedener Sportarten, Singen, Spielen musikalischer Instrumente. Der Lehrer kommentiert jedes Bild mit *I'd like to be able to ...* Anschließend versuchen die Schüler in Einzel- oder Partnerarbeit sich vorzustellen, was die Personen auf dem Arbeitsblatt wohl denken könnten. Dabei benutzen sie die Struktur *I'd like to be able to ...* Für das jeweilige Bild kann es durchaus verschiedene Antworten geben.

● Lösungen
1. *I'd like to be able to drive/to buy a car.*
2. *I'd like to be able to play (football) like that.*
3. *I'd like to be able to buy new clothes.*
4. *I'd like to be able to skate.*
5. *I'd like to be able to sing like that.*
6. *I'd like to be able to use that/a computer.*
7. *I'd like to be able to swim.*
8. *I'd like to be able to dance.*

Nach dem Vorlesen ihrer Antworten notieren die Schüler einige Fähigkeiten, die sie gerne besäßen. Sie sollten ermutigt werden, nach unbekanntem Wortschatz zu suchen bzw. zu fragen.

2. What will or won't we be able to do?
In Gruppenarbeit und unter Verwendung der vorgegebenen Strukturen schreiben die Lernenden auf, wie sie sich die Welt in hundert Jahren vorstellen.

● Mögliche Antworten
People/They/Everybody will/might be able to
– *live on other planets*
– *go on trips to the moon*
– *fly everywhere very cheaply*
– *travel much faster*

- *use computers*
- *learn/work at home*
- *use machines for nearly everything*
- *speak two languages*
- *use the TV for shopping*
- *go shopping any time*
- *watch thousands of TV channels* usw.

They won't/might not be able to drive cars into towns,
- *swim in the sea (pollution),*
- *go skiing in the Alps (global warming)*
- *use money, only cards*
- *buy newspapers, they'll be on TV*
- *buy books, they'll be on cassettes* usw.

A 16

Be allowed to

Die Struktur *be allowed to* wird in dieser Einheit nur in ihrer Passivverwendung geübt und nicht in der Aktivform *to allow someone to do something.*

1. If you saw these signs would you understand them?
Die abgebildeten Verbotszeichen können im Klassenverband, in Einzel-, Partner- oder Gruppenarbeit versprachlicht werden.

● Lösungen
1. *You're not allowed to park here.*
2. *You're not allowed to smoke here.*
3. *You're not allowed to go through here.*
4. *You're not allowed to go out of here.*
5. *You're not allowed to take dogs in here.*
6. *You're not allowed to take photos in here.*
7. *You're not allowed to go faster than 30.*
8. *You're not allowed to walk on the grass.*

2. At school
Mit einem Partner oder in Gruppen schreiben die Schüler drei Dinge auf, die sie in der Schule nicht tun dürfen. Folgende Wortschatzhilfe kann gegeben werden: *run, stand on, listen to, eat, fight* usw.

● Mögliche Antworten
We're not allowed to run in the classrooms, corridors/run around in school; stand, jump on the desks/listen to walkmen/eat in lessons/fight/go to sleep/write on the desks/jump out of the windows/chew chewing gum/bring pets to school.

Imagine you are the head teacher of a school ...
In Gruppen stellen die Schüler als fiktive Schulleiter zwei Listen der Dinge zusammen, die ihren Schülern erlaubt und nicht erlaubt werden. Die Listen können auch lustige Dinge enthalten, z. B.
Pupils are allowed to bring pets to school/have parties/dance on the desks/ ...
Pupils aren't allowed to do any homework, tests/work hard/write anything/ ...

3. At home
Die Ge- und Verbote, die die Schüler am eigenen Leibe zu Hause erfahren, können distanzierter betrachtet werden, wenn sich die Lernenden vorstellen, sie hätten selbst die Fürsorgepflicht für junge Leute in ihrem eigenen Alter. Wiederum bleibt die Struktur auf die Passivform beschränkt. Wie in der vorausgegangenen Übung ist es sinnvoll, die Schüler in Gruppen ihre Ideen zusammenstellen zu lassen. Fortgeschrittenere Lerner könnten anschließend über die Listen diskutieren.

A 17

Might

1. What might happen?
Die Bilder dienen als Sprechimpuls für die Struktur *might (not).* Sie können mündlich und/oder schriftlich, in Einzel- oder Partnerarbeit verbalisiert werden.

● Lösungen
1. *She might not come.*
2. *He might not ring (me).*
3. *They might be late.*
4. *They might give me one.*
5. *They might not see me.*
6. *He might fall off his bike.*
7. *He might buy a car.*

2. What about you?
In einem zweiten Schritt verwenden die Lernenden die Struktur *might (not),* um über sich selbst zu sprechen bzw. zu schreiben.

A 18

Might/could have

In dem in dieser Unit zu übenden Sprechakt (es hätte etwas passieren können) gibt es kaum einen Unterschied zwischen *might have* und *could have.* Um die Strukturen zu üben, beschreiben die Schüler mündlich und/oder schriftlich, in Einzel-, Gruppen- oder Partnerarbeit die Abbildungen.

● Lösungen
The next day he crossed the road/street without looking. He might/could have had an accident, but he didn't.
The day after that he fell off his bike. He might/could have broken something, but he didn't.
On Monday he ate some old cheese. He might/could have been ill, but he wasn't.
On Tuesday he left some tablets on the table. His sister might/could have eaten them, but she didn't.
On Wednesday he forgot to meet his aunt at the station. She might/could have been very angry, but she wasn't.
On Thursday he forgot to deliver the newspapers. He might/could have lost his job, but he didn't.
On Friday he left his jacket on the bus. He might/could have lost it, but he didn't.
On Saturday he left some money on his desk. Someone might/could have taken/stolen it, but they didn't.
On Sunday he left the budgie's cage open. It might/could have flown away, but it didn't.

On Monday he put his glasses on a chair. Someone might/could have sat on them, but they didn't.
On Tuesday he fed a monkey at the zoo. It might/could have bitten him, but it didn't.

A 19

Must/can't have

In dieser Einheit werden die Strukturen *must have* und *can't have* mit der Funktion „logische Schlussfolgerungen ziehen" verdeutlicht und geübt.

1. What does this house tell you?
In Partner- oder Gruppenarbeit ziehen die Schüler unter Verwendung der angegebenen Strukturen Schlüsse über die Lebensgewohnheiten der bisherigen Bewohner des abgebildeten Hauses.

● Lösungen
They/Someone must have:
- *smoked (cigarettes)*
- *drunk a lot of/liked coffee*
- *been interested in/liked/watched a lot of films*
- *eaten/had a lot of sweets*
- *eaten a lot of/liked fast food*
- *had a child*
- *had a budgie*
- *played tennis*
- *played football*
- *painted (pictures)*

They can't have:
- *cleaned the windows (very often/for a long time)*
- *had much time for/done much cooking/enjoyed cooking very much*
- *had much time for the garden/gardening/liked gardening very much*
- *used the garage/had a car*

2. Jokes
In Gruppen oder mit einem Partner vervollständigen die Schüler die Witze entweder durch Hinzufügen von *must be* oder *must have.*

● Lösungen
1. *His fingers must be tired!*
2. *… I must have cut you.*
3. *… so it must be.*
4. *This café must have a very clean kitchen.*

A 20

Need not

In der ersten Übung wird *need not* im Präsens geübt, in der zweiten im *simple past (didn't need to)* und in der dritten Übung in der Zukunft *(will/won't need to).*

1. An African family
Ein Vergleich zwischen dem Lebensstil westeuropäischer Menschen und dem einer afrikanischen Bauernfamilie macht den Lernenden bewusst, dass sie viele beschwerliche, das bloße Überleben garantierende Dinge nicht mehr zu tun brauchen.
Der Eingangstext lässt sich anhand des auf dem OHP erscheinenden Bildes einführen, z. B.:

L: *Where do you think these people live?* (Nach einigen Schülervorschlägen): *Well, they live in Africa.* (Beschreibt das obige Bild) *This is Miriam. She's thirteen. This is her brother Nelson. He's ten. And here are Miriam's mother and father.*
Their life is very hard. In the pictures you can see some of the things they have to do. For example, they have to …?

Schülervorschläge: *Work in the fields/get water from the river/Miriam has to carry the water on her head/They have to wash their clothes in the river.*

Danach wird der Text gelesen (vom Lehrer, von Schülern oder durch stilles Lesen). Die anschließende Übung eignet sich für Gruppen- oder Partnerarbeit: mithilfe der angegebenen Struktur vergleichen die Schüler ihren Lebensstil mit dem der afrikanischen Familie, wobei sie Tätigkeiten aufschreiben, die sie und ihre Familienmitglieder nicht zu verrichten brauchen. Die Lernenden können hinzufügen, wie die entsprechenden Tätigkeiten bei ihnen zu Hause aussehen. Dazu sind folgende Wortschatzangaben hilfreich: *buy, shops, washing machines, bathrooms, homes, bikes, cars, go by bus, cooker, microwaves, more than one room, floor, go to school, play.*
Eine Ergänzung könnte wie folgt lauten: *My mother doesn't need to make our clothes. We buy them in shops.*

● Mögliche Aussagen
My father/brother doesn't need to/needn't work in the fields all day.
My mother doesn't need to/needn't make all our clothes – we buy them in shops.
My mother doesn't need to/We don't need to/needn't/wash our clothes in a river – we have (a) washing machine(s).
We don't need to/needn't wash in rivers – we have bathrooms.
We don't need to/needn't go and get water from rivers – we have it in our homes.
We don't need to/needn't carry things on our heads – we use bikes, cars and buses.
My sister doesn't need to/needn't make a fire/sell things in the market/work.
We don't need to/needn't make fires for cooking – we have/use cookers and microwaves.
We don't need to/needn't walk everywhere. We ride bikes or go by car or bus.
We don't need to/needn't/live and sleep in one room. We have more than one room in our homes.
We don't need to/needn't sleep on the floor.
Children don't need to/needn't work. They can go to school and play.

2. A hundred years ago
Nach dem Vergleich mit dem zeitgenössischen afrikanischen Lebensstil vergleichen die Lernenden ihre eigene Lebensweise mit der ihrer Landsleute von vor hundert Jahren. Die Gruppen- oder Partnerarbeit kann zunächst ohne Hilfe des angegebenen Wortschatzes versucht werden.

● Lösungen
People/They/Children didn't need to learn so many things/learn to drive, use computers

They didn't need to go everywhere by car/travel far to work/buy new things all the time/use so many machines/so much electricity, water, energy
Children didn't need to stay at school for so long/do so much homework/so many tests/ …
Fortgeschrittenere Schüler können versuchen, die Lösungsvorschläge zu ergänzen und zu diskutieren.

3. And the future?
Wiederum in Gruppen oder mit einem Partner versuchen die Schüler, zunächst mit zugedeckten Wortschatzangaben Prognosen für die Zukunft aufzustellen. Neben der Angabe der Struktur kann der Lehrer schon bestimmte Themenbereiche antippen, z. B. *Think about school, work, life at home. Think about robots and computers.*

● Mögliche Antworten
won't
Children/Pupils won't need to
– *go to school. They'll learn at home with computers.*
– *write on paper. They'll use computers.*
They won't need to build schools.
People won't need to go to work. They'll work at home.
People won't need to go to work five days a week.
They won't need to cook/clean. Robots will do it./We'll eat pills.
They won't need to go shopping. They'll do it by phoning/over the phone.
They won't need to buy newspapers. They'll read them on computers.
They won't need to post letters. They'll use fax machines.

will
Everyone will need to have a computer at home/speak English/learn more than one job/live in/travel to different places for their jobs/save electricity, water, energy/stay out of the sun/inside because the sun will be too hot/ …

A 21

Should

1. Thinking about young people
Als Einstieg wird ein allgemeines Gespräch über junge Leute geführt, wobei unbekannte Vokabeln des folgenden Fragebogens vorweggenommen werden.
In Partnerarbeit wird dann der Fragebogen bearbeitet. Zuerst liest Partner A alle Aussagen vor und notiert durch Ankreuzen die Antworten seines Partners. Dann werden die Rollen vertauscht. Anschließend lesen einzelne Schüler einige ausgewählte Antworten vor. Es ist hilfreich, folgendes Antwortmuster anzugeben: *She thinks/doesn't think …*
S1: (Sabine) *thinks there should be more places for young people to go. She doesn't think young people should stay at school as long as they can.*
usw.

2. My ideas
In Einzel- oder Partnerarbeit schreiben die Schüler einige eigene Ideen über junge Menschen auf. Im Klassenverband können die Vorschläge ergänzt und diskutiert werden.

3. What I would like
Im Klassenverband, in Partner- oder Gruppenarbeit, mündlich oder schriftlich machen sich die Lernenden Gedanken über ihre Idealpartner und ihren idealen Wohnort. Folgender Wortschatz kann angegeben werden: *My ideal boy/girlfriend: good-looking, kind, interested in, like …ing, like my friends, be able to, good at, have the same interests as me, lots of friends, have a sense of humour/ …*
The place I would like to live in should be near the sea, in the country, a big city, in (America), people from lots of different countries, be hot, have lots of things to do, a swimming pool, nice architecture, a river, parks/ …

A 22

Should have

What a holiday!
Als Einstieg schildert der Lehrer Situationen, in denen er irrtümlicherweise etwas Unkluges getan oder etwas Wichtiges unterlassen hat. Die Situationen können sich z. B. auf den Schulalltag (1) oder auf die Ferien beziehen (2). Die im Demonstrationsgespräch unterstrichenen Ausdrücke erscheinen an der Tafel oder auf dem OHP. Während dieser Phase wird die nachfolgende Übung von unbekanntem Wortschatz vorentlastet. Auf die Kurzformen in der Aussprache von [ˈʃʊdəv] und [ˈʃʊdəntəv] sollte Wert gelegt werden.

(1) L: *You know, I was late this morning. My alarm clock didn't go off/work, so I was in a hurry. I should have fed the cat, but I didn't have time. And I left all the windows open. I shouldn't have done that. I hope nobody breaks in. I left some money on the table. I know I shouldn't have left it there, but I just didn't have time. I should have watered my flowers, too …*

(2) L: *Do you ever do some really silly things? I do. Do you know what happened/I did the last time I went on holiday? I forgot to do lots of things. The first thing was that one of my bags didn't arrive at the hotel. I should have put my name and address on it, but I didn't. It arrived on the day I went home. And the other bag was far too heavy. I shouldn't have taken so many clothes. Then I forgot about the money. I should have changed money, but I forgot …*
This is what happened to some other people. They went on holiday and forgot to do lots of things.

Nach dem anschließenden Vorlesen des Anfangstextes und der beiden Beispielsätze versuchen die Schüler in Einzel- oder Partnerarbeit die Bilder zu beschreiben.
Wenn nötig, kann die Bedeutung der Struktur wie folgt erklärt werden: *should have* und *shouldn't have* für Verpflichtungen, denen man nicht nachgekommen ist.

● Lösungen
1. *She shouldn't have brought so many clothes.*
2. *He should have changed his money.*
3. *He should have checked when the banks are open.*
4. *She shouldn't have been in the sun for so long.*
5. *She shouldn't have walked about in the rain.*
6. *They should have bought a map.*
7. *He shouldn't have gone swimming there.*
8. *He shouldn't have eaten so much ice-cream.*
9. *He should have learned the language.*

10. *They shouldn't have left the window open.*
11. *They shouldn't have left money on the table.*
12. *They should have watered the flowers.*
13. *They should have told the postman about their holiday.*
14. *They shouldn't have left things in the fridge.*

A 23

Would like

Die Übungen dieser Einheit konzentrieren sich auf die Fragestruktur Fragewort + *would you like to …?*

1. Where would you like to go?
Als Einstieg wird das bereits vorhandene Wissen der Lernenden über englischsprachige Länder aktiviert: in welchen Ländern wird Englisch gesprochen, was gibt es dort an Hauptsehenswürdigkeiten?
In einem zweiten Schritt schreiben die Schüler auf, in welches bzw. welche dieser Länder sie gern reisen möchten und was sie dort unternehmen würden, z. B.:
I'd like to go to/see America.
I'd go and see the Grand Canyon.
I'd visit/have a look at Hollywood.
I'd also like to see India.
usw.
Anschließend lesen einige Schüler ihre Aussagen vor.

2. Ask your classmates and write their answers down
Im Klassenverband stellen die Schüler turnusmäßig die zwei Fragen:
Where would you like to go (and) what would you do there?
Die Antworten werden gesammelt, um ein Klassenprofil zu erstellen. Die Schüler sollten bei ihren Antworten nicht zu unnatürlichen, ganzen Sätzen gezwungen werden. Die einzig natürliche Antwort zum Beispiel auf die Frage *Where would you like to go?* ist *America/India* usw. Über die Ergebnisse des Klassenprofils kann abschließend diskutiert werden.

3. Tell me
Die Lernenden stellen Frage- und Antwortkarten her, auf denen die Fragestruktur Fragewort + *would you like to …?* sowie vier Auswahlantworten stehen. Außer den vorgegebenen Fragen gibt es zahlreiche andere Möglichkeiten, z. B. *What would you like for lunch? Which film/book would you like to see/read? Who would you like to be? Where would you like to live?* Fortgeschrittenere Schüler können nach folgendem vorgegebenen Muster sowohl Fragen als auch Auswahlantworten selbst erfinden:
Where/What/Which/Who would you like to …?
Die Fragen werden entweder im Klassenverband oder in Gruppen gestellt.

Weiterführendes Projekt
In einem weiterführenden Projekt können die Lernenden Informationen über die wichtigsten Sehenswürdigkeiten in englischsprachigen Ländern sammeln (Bibliotheken, Reiseprospekte, Werbevideos).

A 24

Want/would like

Bei diesem Arbeitsblatt wird das Gewicht auf folgende Strukturen gelegt:
Aussagesätze:
I (don't) want a career/to have children.
I'd like a career/to have children.
I wouldn't like a career/to have children.

Fragesätze:
What do you want?
What don't you want?
Um eine Überforderung zu vermeiden, werden die Frageformen *(What) would you like …?* und *What wouldn't you like?* zu diesem Zeitpunkt weggelassen.

1. What teenagers want
Die unterschiedliche Bedeutung von *want* und *would like* wird mithilfe einer Statistik über die stark und weniger stark ausgeprägten Wünsche Heranwachsender verdeutlicht. Die Statistik kann im Klassenverband, in Einzel-, Partner- oder Gruppenarbeit, mündlich und/oder schriftlich versprachlicht werden.

● Lösungen
Eighteen per cent want a career.
Twelve per cent would like a career.
Forty per cent don't want a career.
Thirty per cent wouldn't like a career.
Forty-two per cent want lots of money.
usw.
In fortgeschritteneren Klassen kann über diese Zahlen diskutiert werden.

2. What about you and your classmates?
Der abgebildete Modelldialog dient als Impuls für ein Partnergespräch, in dem abwechselnd jeder Partner die Fragen stellt: *What do you want and what don't you want in life?* Je nach Klasse kann sich die Antwort, die schriftlich festgehalten werden soll, auf die zwei Strukturen *I (really) want* und *I don't want* beschränken oder auch weitere beinhalten *(I'd hate, I'd (quite) like, I wouldn't like (very much))*. Zusätzlich zur Verwendung des vorgeschlagenen Wortschatzes sollten die Schüler dazu ermutigt werden, nach unbekannten Wörtern zu fragen bzw. zu suchen. Auf die Gefahr der Verwechselung von deutschem „will“ mit englischem *will* sollte aufmerksam gemacht werden, siehe Merkkästchen.
Tell the class about you and your partner
Anschließend werden die Gesprächsergebnisse der Klasse berichtet, z. B.:
I (really) want …
I'd (quite) like …
I don't want/would hate …
wouldn't like …
(Axel) (really) wants …
He'd (quite) like …
He doesn't want/would hate …
He wouldn't like … (very much)

3. Make a class survey
Die verschiedenen Einzelaussagen lassen sich zu einem Klassenprofil zusammenfassen, wie auf dem Arbeitsblatt

angedeutet. Die Ergebnisse können schließlich diskutiert werden.

A 25

Want someone to do something

1. Signs and advertisements
Als Einstieg dienen einige allgemeine Bemerkungen über die verschiedenen Funktionen von Werbung:
Some advertisements want people to buy things.
Some want people to give money for something.
Some want people to join an organisation.
And some don't want people to use so much energy, do they?
They want us to use less energy.
Im Klassenverband, in Einzel- oder Partnerarbeit, mündlich und/oder schriftlich werden die Schilder und Werbetexte unter Verwendung der angegebenen Strukturen verbalisiert.

● Lösungen
1. *They want people to put bottles in here.*
2. *They don't want people to pick the flowers.*
3. *They don't want us/people to walk on the grass.*
4. *They don't want people to smoke.*
5. *They want people to buy/use Fab shampoo/look like the girl in the picture.*
6. *They want people to join the WWF/help to save wildlife.*
7. *They want people to use less energy.*
They don't want people to use so much energy.
8. *They don't want people to keep/put birds (and animals) in cages.*
They want people to stop keeping/putting birds (and animals) in cages.
9. *They want people to give money (to help poor children).*
10. *They want people to be quiet.*
They don't want people to talk.
11. *They want people to go to this English language school/learn English at this school/here.*
12. *They want people to stop killing animals to make/for clothes.*
They don't want people to kill animals to make/for clothes.
13. *They want people to adopt a whale/help (to save) whales.*

2. They want me to ...
In Partner- oder Gruppenarbeit und mithilfe der angegebenen Strukturen schreiben die Lernenden auf, was Mitmenschen von ihnen fordern. Zusätzlich zur Verwendung des vorgeschlagenen Wortschatzes sollten die Schüler dazu ermutigt werden, nach unbekannten Wörtern zu fragen bzw. zu suchen.

3. I want them to ...
Der abgebildete Modelldialog dient als Impuls, unter Anwendung der vorgegebenen Strukturen die eigenen Forderungen an andere zu äußern. In fortgeschritteneren Klassen kann anschließend über diese Forderungen diskutiert werden.

4. Your children?
In einem abschließenden Schritt stellen sich die Schüler vor, sie hätten eigene Kinder. Im Klassenverband oder in Gruppen formulieren sie mit Hilfe der vorgeschlagenen Strukturen ihre Erziehungsmaßnahmen.

A 26

Passiv mit simple present

In dieser Einheit wird das Passiv in der *simple present*-Form mit und ohne *by-agent* in einem geeigneten Kontext dargestellt und geübt. Bei der Arbeit mit Passivsätzen sollten grundsätzlich kontextlose Umformungsübungen vom Aktiv ins Passiv vermieden werden, wie etwa:
In Italy many people eat pasta every day.
In Italy pasta is eaten by many people every day.
Die aus solchen Transformationen entstehenden Sätze klingen nicht nur unnatürlich, sondern erwecken bei den Schülern auch den Eindruck, dass es zwischen Aktiv- und Passivsätzen keine inhaltlichen Unterschiede gäbe. Außerdem wird die kommunikative Funktion und Kontextabhängigkeit von Passivkonstruktionen nicht deutlich.

How young people in different parts of the world live
Durch das Thema der Übung sollen Schüler erkennen, dass es zwar ganz andere, aber gleichwertige Lebensgewohnheiten neben den eigenen gibt.
Zur Einstimmung wird in einem allgemeinen Gespräch der Wissensstand der Lernenden zum Thema festgestellt, z. B.: *Do you know that English is spoken in about 45 countries? And they're all very different. Let's think about how people live in different parts of the world. Have you ever read anything about people in different countries? Or seen any TV programmes? For example, the kind of clothes they wear, the types of houses and so on?*
Nach der Einführung in das Thema werden die ersten beiden Textteile *(Clothes, School)* vom Lehrer zweimal vorgelesen oder auf Hörkassette dargeboten. Der schriftliche Text bleibt abgedeckt, und die Schüler versuchen lediglich, den Inhalt global zu erfassen. Beim dritten Vortrag lesen die Schüler den Text mit und versuchen, unbekannten Wortschatz aus dem Zusammenhang zu erschließen.
In einem weiteren Schritt wird die Passivstruktur zusammen mit den Schülern erarbeitet, z. B.:
L: *There's one kind or one form of sentence that is used a lot in these texts. Can you find and underline some examples?*
Die Beispiele werden gesammelt, und es wird zunächst die Form analysiert: *is/are + past participle.* Bei zugedecktem Arbeitsblatt wird dann die Funktion festgestellt:
L: *Why do you think the writer chose this type of sentence? What does it express? When does the writer use "by" and when not?*
Nach einigen Schülerversuchen wird die Aufmerksamkeit auf das auf dem Arbeitsblatt abgebildete Merkkästchen gelenkt.
Während eines vierten Vortrags der ersten beiden Textteile notieren sich die Schüler auf englisch die wichtigsten Informationen, z. B.: *Hot countries – clothes long, thin material. Sari – Indian women.* In Partner-, Gruppen- oder Einzelarbeit wandeln die Schüler ihre Notizen in zusammenhängende, ganze Sätze um. Die erstellten Texte werden der gesamten Klasse vorgelesen.
Analog wird mit den restlichen Textteilen des Arbeitsblattes verfahren.

Zur schriftlichen Übung erstellt der Lehrer einen Lückentext, in den die Passivkonstruktionen einzutragen sind. Je nach Klasse kann der Lückentext entweder aus dem ganzen Text oder nur aus Teilen davon bestehen. Fortgeschrittenere Schüler können versuchen, ohne Hilfe eines Lückentextes und nur anhand ihrer Notizen den Text wiederherzustellen. Anschließend wird er in Selbstkontrolle mit dem Ausgangstext verglichen.
Beispiel für einen Lückentext. Je nach Klasse können auch die Infinitive der zu verwendenden Verben angegeben werden:

Clothes
In hot countries people wear clothes that are long and .... thin material. The sari, for example, ... Indian women.
Sometimes special clothes .... to show that people are in an organisation. In some schools, for example, uniforms ....

School
In some parts of Australia many children live hundreds of kilometres from the nearest school. Lessons .... to them by post and they .... by teachers over the radio. In hot countries children .... often .... outside. In India some children .... to school .... rickshaw. Others walk or go by bus.

Transport
In many countries most people travel by bus. Luggage .... on top of the buses. They .... often .... with pictures and flowers.

Food
Most Chinese and Asian meals .... of rice. This .... with meat or vegetables. Chinese food is mostly vegetables that .... very quickly in a pan. The pan .... a wok. Woks .... for cooking nearly everything in China. The food .... with two sticks, called chopsticks.
In Italy many people eat pasta every day. It is .... flour, water and oil.

Birthdays
Birthdays .... in different ways all over the world. In China one year .... to everyone's age at the Chinese New Year. Birthdays .... only .... at the age of ten, and then every ten years after that. In Switzerland a tree .... when a baby .... , a pear tree for a girl and apple for a boy. On Mexican birthdays a ball .... out of papier maché. It .... a piñata. It .... with small presents.

A 27

Passiv mit present continuous

In dieser Einheit wird die Funktion des Passivs in der *present continuous*-Form verdeutlicht und geübt. Das Thema „bedrohte Tier-, Vogel- und Pflanzenwelt“ knüpft voraussichtlich an Interessen der Lernenden an, ansonsten soll es für die darin angesprochene Problematik sensibilisieren. Kontextlose Umwandlungsübungen von Aktivsätzen in Passivsätze sollten im übrigen grundsätzlich vermieden werden (Begründung vgl. einleitende Lehrerhinweise zum Passiv mit *simple present*).

1. Wildlife in danger
In einem allgemeinen Gespräch wird die Thematik eingeführt und das schon vorhandene Wissen der Schüler zusammengetragen, z. B.:

L: *Can you tell me the names of some animals in English? Have you ever seen any of them? Where? In a field? In a zoo? Or only in pictures? ...*
Today a lot of animals are in danger. (Wenn keine Beispiele aus der Klasse kommen, gibt der Lehrer selber Beispiele vor: *Siberian tiger, otter, chinchilla.*) *Do you know why these animals are in danger?*

Nach der Einführung in die Thematik wird der Text zweimal vom Lehrer vorgelesen bzw. auf Hörkassette dargeboten, wobei die Schüler lediglich versuchen, den Inhalt global zu erfassen. Beim dritten Vortrag lesen die Schüler den Text leise mit und versuchen, unbekannte Wörter aus dem Zusammenhang zu erschließen.
Danach wird die Aufmerksamkeit auf die Passivkonstruktion gelenkt. Bildung und Funktion der Struktur werden mit den Lernenden erarbeitet: *What kind of sentence or structure is used all the time in this text? Underline some examples of it.*
In Partner- oder Gruppenarbeit werden Beispiele gesammelt, und die Form wird beschrieben: *is/are + being + past participle.*
Zur Erarbeitung der Funktion sollten die Arbeitsblätter zugedeckt bleiben:
Why does the writer use passive sentences? What does that show? When does the writer use "by ..." and when not?
Nach einigen Deutungsversuchen wird die Aufmerksamkeit auf das Merkkästchen gelenkt.

2. Informing other people
In Gruppen- oder Partnerarbeit erstellen die Schüler Poster, um Mitschüler über bedrohte Tierarten zu informieren. Das Arbeitsblatt kann als Vorlage für größere Poster dienen, die anschließend in der Schule ausgehängt werden.

● Lösungen
Did you know that all the time many wonderful animals, birds and plants are disappearing from the earth?
Some are being killed because they are beautiful.
Birds are being taken from South America(n forests).
They are being put into cages as pets.
Butterflies are being collected.
Plants are being taken and sold (as house plants).
Animals and birds are (even) being killed for "sport".
Rain forests are being cut down.
The wood is being sold and exported.
The land is being used by farmers.
Wildlife is also disappearing because more and more roads, shops, houses and car parks are being built.
Wild, natural land is being made into farmland.
And so the wildlife that lived there is being destroyed.
Many animals, birds and plants are also being killed by chemicals in the rivers, the land and the atmosphere.

3. What can be done?
In Partner- oder Gruppenarbeit werden Vorschläge dazu gesammelt, wie dem Natursterben Einhalt geboten werden kann, z. B.:

We shouldn't buy/wear/use animals/animal furs, skins for decoration/clothes/souvenirs.
- *buy/keep/collect animals, birds, plants from the forests*
- *take away/destroy the places where animals, birds and plants live*
- *put so many chemicals into the rivers ...*
- *build too many ...*

We should stop buying furs/skins/wood/animals/birds and plants that people have taken from the forests
- *destroying places where ... live*
- *cutting the rain forests down*
- *building so many ...*

We should join an organisation to help wildlife.

We should stop people from ...
- *taking wildlife from the forests*
- *killing/buying animals and birds for decoration/sport*
- *cutting the rain forests down*

Adressen für weitere Informationen:
WWF (World Wide Fund for Nature)
Freepost
Panda House
Godalming
Surrey GU7 1BR
England

Friends of the Earth
26/28 Underwood St
London N1 7JQ
England

A 28

Passiv mit simple past

In dieser Einheit werden sowohl Passivsätze im *simple past* mit und ohne *by-agent* als auch die Stellung des Zeitadverbs bzw. Adjektivs *first* geübt:

*The first ... **was/were made** by ...*
*... **was/were first made** by ...*

Kontextlose Umwandlungsübungen von Aktivsätzen in Passivsätze sollten grundsätzlich vermieden werden (Begründung vgl. einleitende Lehrerhinweise zum Passiv mit *simple present*).

1. How much do you know?
Als Einstieg in das Thema „Erfindungen" kann man über alltägliche Gebrauchsgegenstände sprechen und die Schüler über deren erstes Auftreten spekulieren lassen, z. B.:

L: *Who has a computer/telephone/walkman/TV/ ... at home? Did people always have these things? When do you think the first (computer/ ...) was made/used? What about toothpaste? And biros? Can you guess?*

Nach einigen Rateversuchen wird die Information vom Lehrer gegeben (s. Arbeitsblatt). Das Blatt wird noch nicht ausgeteilt, damit die Regeln für die Bildung und Anwendung des Passivs zusammen mit den Lernenden erarbeitet werden können.
Die das Arbeitsblatt einleitenden zwei Modellsätze werden an die Tafel geschrieben, worauf die Schüler zu erklären versuchen, warum in den Sätzen das Passiv – einmal mit und einmal ohne *by* ... – verwendet wurde (s. Merkkasten):

*Toothpaste **was first used** in 1841.*
*The first biros **were made** by a Hungarian.*

In Partner- oder Gruppenarbeit werden die Lückensätze vervollständigt und der Klasse vorgelesen. Dabei nehmen die Schüler etwaige Verbesserungen auf ihrem eigenen Arbeitsblatt selbst vor.

● Lösungen
1. *The earliest numbers were written about 5,000 years ago.*
2. *The first alphabet was used in Syria about 3,500 years ago.*
3. *The first Christmas card was sent in 1853.*
4. *Paper was first produced by the Chinese in 105 AD.*
5. *The first biros were made by Lazlo Biro from Hungary.*
6. *Pencils were first made in the 1790s in France and England.*
7. *Felt-tips were first used by the Japanese in 1964.*
8. *Personal computers were first sold in the 1970s.*
9. *Plastic was first produced in 1862.*
10. *The first watch was made by a Bavarian in 1504.*
11. *The first bar of chocolate was made in 1819.*
12. *Tobacco was first smoked by the American Indians. It was brought to Europe in the 1500s.*
13. *Movies were first seen in New York in 1885.*

2. A quiz
Die Klasse wird in zwei Mannschaften, *team* A und B, eingeteilt. Vier Schüler aus jeder Mannschaft gehen nach vorne und bilden jeweils eine Quizrunde *(panel)*, die Fragen der jeweiligen Gegenmannschaft zu beantworten hat. Die Mannschaften bekommen einige Minuten Zeit, um sich geeignete Fragen auszudenken. Die Fragen nehmen die in der ersten Übung gelieferten Informationen auf, geben sie jedoch inhaltlich teils richtig, teils absichtlich falsch wieder, wie auf dem Arbeitsblatt vorgeschlagen. Die Fragen werden abwechselnd von verschiedenen Sprechern der Mannschaften A und B vorgetragen.
Die jeweils vier Teilnehmer der beiden Quizrunden arbeiten zusammen und versuchen, die in den Fragen enthaltene Information als richtig oder falsch zu erkennen und ggf. zu korrigieren. Für jede richtige Antwort und für jede richtige Korrektur gibt es je einen Punkt, z. B.:

A *(team)*: *The first alphabet was used 3,500 years ago. Is that right or wrong?*
B *(panel)*: *That's right.* (1 Punkt)
B *(team)*: *Pencils were first made in the nineteen hundreds.*
A *(panel, S 1)*: *That's wrong.* (1 Punkt) *They were made earlier, but I can't remember when.*
A *(panel, S 2)*: *Were they made in the 1890s?*

Wenn die Teilnehmer der zuerst befragten Quizrunde (hier A) die Frage nicht beantworten können oder falsch beantworten, geht das Antwortrecht an die andere Quizrunde (hier B):

L: *No, they weren't made in the 1890s. What about panel B? Do you know?*
B *(panel)*: *Was it in the 1790s?*
L: *That's right. One point for you. The next question please – from team A.*
A *(team)*: *Felt-tips ...* usw.

Nach 3–4 Fragen werden die Teilnehmer der beiden Quizrunden ausgewechselt.

A 29

Passiv mit present perfect

Das Passiv in der *present perfect*-Form steht häufig am Anfang einer Nachrichtensendung, z. B. im Radio, im Fernsehen oder in Zeitungen. Die anschließenden Details werden in der *simple past*-Form vorgetragen. Damit bietet sich die Textsorte Schlagzeilen geradezu an zur Erarbeitung der vorliegenden Struktur. Kontextlose Umwandlungsübungen von Aktivsätzen in Passivsätze sollten im Übrigen grundsätzlich vermieden werden (Begründung vgl. einleitende Lehrerhinweise zum Passiv mit *simple present*).

1. Headlines
Um die Textsorte Schlagzeilen zu veranschaulichen, sollten ein paar englischsprachige Zeitungen mitgebracht werden. Die die Einheit einleitenden vier Schlagzeilen werden im Klassenverband ausformuliert.

● Lösungen
2. *A film star has been killed in an accident.*
3. *300 toys have been collected by (some) pupils for a children's home.*
4. *A baby has been found in the woods by a dog.*

Anschließend werden Bildung und Funktion des *present perfect*-Passivs erarbeitet (vgl. Merkkästchen).

2. Explain in more detail what these headlines tell us
Die Schlagzeilen werden in Einzel- oder Partnerarbeit mündlich oder schriftlich ausformuliert.

● Lösungen
1. *Two baby gorillas have been born in a zoo.*
2. *A girl has been given a medal for saving a child.*
3. *A bestseller has been written by a schoolboy.*
4. *Two thirds of the rain forests have been cut down in three years.*
5. *A film has been made by schoolchildren.*
6. *The city centre has been closed to cars.*
7. *The world chess record has been broken by a computer.*
8. *A youth club has been opened in an old factory.*
9. *A trip round the world has been won by a 15-year-old.*
10. *The race has been won by Oxford.*
11. *Some paintings have been stolen by a cleaner.*
12. *Six people have been taken to hospital after a train crash.*

A 30

Passiv mit will-Futur

In dieser Einheit wird das Passiv in der *will/won't*-Futurform geübt. Kontextlose Umwandlungsübungen von Aktivsätzen in Passivsätze sollten grundsätzlich vermieden werden (Begründung vgl. einleitende Lehrerhinweise zum Passiv mit *simple present*).

1. Life in a hundred years' time
Zur Einstimmung in das Thema *Life in a hundred years' time* werden Schülerprognosen für die Zukunft gesammelt, wobei der in Übung 1 enthaltene unbekannte Wortschatz schon eingeführt werden kann, z. B.:

L: *When your parents were at school it was very different. And when your children go to school it will be different for them, too. What do you think school will be like in a hundred years' time? Do you think children will still be taught by teachers? Or by robots? Or by computers?*

Als Hilfestellung werden die Strukturen ... *will/won't* ... an die Tafel geschrieben. Nach einigen Schülerbeiträgen wird das Arbeitsblatt ausgeteilt. In Einzel-, Partner- oder Gruppenarbeit tragen die Schüler bei jedem Satz entweder R oder W ein. Anschließend werden die Ergebnisse der ganzen Klasse bekanntgegeben:

L: *Let's see what you think school will be like in a hundred years' time.*
S1: *(I think) children won't be taught by teachers, but by machines.*
L: *I see. And what about the rest of you? What do you think?*
S2: *I think so, too.*
S3: *That's wrong/I don't agree/disagree.* (Fortgeschrittenere Schüler können ihre eigenen Ideen zum Ausdruck bringen).

Als Hilfestellung für die Antworten können folgende Strukturen angegeben werden:

I think ... won't/will ...	*I think so, too.*
I don't think ... will ...	*I don't think so/don't agree/disagree*

2. Write down some of your ideas about the future
In Partner- oder Gruppenarbeit schreiben die Schüler mithilfe der angegebenen Strukturen einige eigene Ideen über die Zukunft auf.

A 31

Passiv mit modalen Hilfsverben

Anhand zweier Worträtsel werden Passivkonstruktionen mit den modalen Hilfsverben *can, have to, must, should* geübt. Kontextlose Umwandlungsübungen von Aktivsätzen in Passivsätze und umgekehrt sollten grundsätzlich vermieden werden (Begründung vgl. einleitende Lehrerhinweise zum Passiv mit *simple present*).

1. A word puzzle
Das erste Worträtsel ruft die Passivkonstruktionen mit modalen Hilfsverben noch einmal in Erinnerung. Die Lösungen werden im Klassenverband oder in Partnerarbeit gefunden. Das Merkkästchen verdeutlicht die Bildung der verschiedenen Strukturen.

● Lösungen
2. *Tea*
3. *Hamburger*
4. *Soup*

2. Now you make up the clues
In Partner- oder Gruppenarbeit werden die *clues* unter Anwendung der zu übenden Strukturen vervollständigt.

● Lösungen
1. *It should be eaten every day. (Fruit)*
2. *It can be sold in bottles or cartons. (Milk)*
3. *It can't be bought in a bottle. (Bread)*
4. *In Britain it has to be bought at the chemist's. (Aspirin)*
5. *They mustn't/shouldn't/can't be sold to children. (Cigarettes)*
6. *They can be bought at British post offices. (Postcards)*
7. *They have to/must be used in Britain. (Pounds)*
8. *It has to/must be worn in some British schools. (Uniform)*
9. *They can be made of plastic or wood. (Desks)*
10. *It shouldn't/mustn't be left on your desk. (Money)*
11. *They should be worn by bike riders. (Helmets)*
12. *They mustn't/can't be ridden on motorways. (Bikes)*
13. *They mustn't/can't be taken onto planes. (Knives)*
14. *They mustn't/can't be taken into Britain. (Animals)*
15. *They should be taken on a walking holiday. (Maps)*
16. *They have to/must be taken for walks every day. (Dogs)*
17. *It can be played outside or inside. (Football)*
18. *It has to/must be played by two teams. (Basketball)*

In Gruppen können die Schüler versuchen, unter Anwendung der zu übenden Strukturen ihre eigenen Kreuzworträtsel zu erstellen. Die fertigen Rätsel werden innerhalb der Gruppen ausgetauscht, so dass jede Gruppe ein ihr unbekanntes Rätsel zu lösen hat.

A 32

Reflexivpronomen, rückbezüglicher Gebrauch: -self, -selves

Eine bekannte Fehlerquelle für deutsche Schüler sind deutsche Reflexivkonstruktionen, denen im Englischen ein einfaches Verb entspricht. Sie werden in dieser Einheit wiederholt und geübt.
Für den hervorhebenden Gebrauch der Reflexivpronomen vgl. Arbeitsblatt 33.

1. Is it worth it?
Zur Einführung des Textes stellt der Lehrer die Frage *Have you ever wondered – ever thought: Is it all worth it? You do something, you work very hard at something, and then you wonder, "Why do I do all this?"* (Gleichzeitig werden *to wonder* und *to be worth it* eingeführt). *I'm going to tell/play you a story about a boy who often wonders, "Is it worth it?" Listen.*
Der Text wird zweimal vom Lehrer vorgelesen bzw. auf Hörkassette dargeboten. Dabei sollen ihn die Schüler lediglich global verstehen können. Beim dritten Vortrag versuchen die Lernenden, unbekannte Wörter aus dem Zusammenhang zu erschließen.

2. What do they say?
Um den Gebrauch der Reflexivpronomen zu festigen, werden in Einzel- oder Partnerarbeit Lückensätze ausgefüllt.
1. *Steve has made himself a training plan …*
2. *In the mornings, when her children have gone to school, Steve's mother makes herself a cup of tea and reads the newspaper.*
3. *Steve's mother worries a lot about her children. They tell her, "Don't worry, Mum. We can look after ourselves".*
4. *Steve is telling his friend what happened yesterday – "I burned/burnt myself on the toaster."*
5. *Steve's little sister is cutting bread. Steve warns her, "Don't cut yourself".*
6. *Steve and his friend are invited to a party. His mother says, "Bye. Enjoy yourselves".*

3. Translate into English
Zur Verdeutlichung der fehlerträchtigen Tatsache, dass etlichen deutschen Reflexivkonstruktionen im Englischen ein einfaches Verb entspricht, bietet sich eine Übersetzungsübung an. Zunächst versuchen die Schüler, in Partner- oder Gruppenarbeit und ohne Hilfe des Einführungstextes zu übersetzen. Erst nach Beendigung der Übersetzung schauen sich die Lernenden den Text an.

● Lösungen
1. *Steve often wonders if it is really worth it.*
2. *His girlfriend complains that he is away so often.*
3. *In the mornings Steve has to hurry.*
4. *Just after eight he has a wash/washes and dresses/gets dressed for school.*
5. *After school Steve often feels very tired.*
6. *Sometimes he lies down for half an hour.*
7. *In the evenings he relaxes.*
8. *He often listens to music.*
9. *Sometimes he imagines he has won an Olympic medal/ a medal at the Olympics/Olympic Games.*

Underline the reflexive verbs in the German sentences and the English verbs you used to translate them.

fragt sich/sich fragen	–	*wonders/to wonder*
beklagt sich	–	*complains*
sich beeilen	–	*hurry*
wäscht … sich	–	*washes*
zieht sich … an	–	*dresses*
fühlt sich	–	*feels*
legt … sich … hin	–	*lies down*
entspannt … sich	–	*relaxes*
hört sich … an	–	*listens to*
stellt sich … vor	–	*imagines*

4. Fill in this table with verbs from text 1 and your translations
In Partner- oder Gruppenarbeit wird die Tabelle mit Verben aus Text und Übersetzungsübung ausgefüllt.

● Lösungen

English verbs – not reflexive	German verbs – reflexive
wonder	sich fragen
imagine	sich vorstellen
complain	sich beschweren
wash	sich waschen
dress	sich anziehen
sit down	sich (hin)setzen
hurry	sich beeilen
feel	sich fühlen
lie down	sich hinlegen
relax	sich entspannen
listen to sth.	sich etwas anhören

A 33

Reflexivpronomen, verstärkender Gebrauch: -self, -selves

Um den verstärkenden oder hervorhebenden Gebrauch der Reflexivpronomen wieder in Erinnerung zu rufen, bringt der Lehrer einige selbstgemachte Gegenstände mit:

L: *Look, I want to show you this* (z. B. Pullover). *A friend of mine made it herself. And this* (z. B. Bild). *Another friend painted this picture himself. Do you like it?*
Do you make things yourselves? Do you make your clothes yourselves? Or your family? Do they make things themselves?

Folgende Strukturen können als Hilfestellung angeschrieben werden:

I ... myself	*make my clothes, birthday cards*
My (sister) ... herself/himself	*make bread*
My parents ... themselves.	*do the decorating/ wallpapering*
	paint the house
	mend bike, watch ...
	wash car
	cut hair
	develop photos

1. Simon Cox, 20 years
Im Anschluß an die Einführung wird das Gespräch auf Menschen gelenkt, die Schwierigkeiten haben, sich selbst zu versorgen, wie z. B. Behinderte. Dabei wird der Text der ersten Übung durch Verwendung eventuell unbekannter Vokabeln vorentlastet:

L: *Some people can't do all these things themselves, can they?*
They need help. What sort of people need help?
S1: *Handicapped people.* (Bemerkung: Bezeichnungen wie *'the handicapped/old/rich'* werden im britischen Englisch zunehmend durch *'handicapped/old/rich people'* ersetzt).
S2: *Old people.*
L: *Yes. Let's think for a moment about handicapped people – people, for instance, who have to live in wheelchairs. What sort of problems might they have?*
(Die Struktur *They can't always ... themselves* wird angegeben).
S3: *They can't always get up themselves.*
S4: *They can't always do their shopping themselves.*
usw.

Nun wird der von Simon Cox handelnde Text zweimal vom Lehrer vorgelesen bzw. auf Hörkassette dargeboten. Die Schüler versuchen lediglich, den Inhalt global zu erfassen. Beim dritten Vortrag lesen die Lernenden den Text mit und versuchen, unbekannte Wörter aus dem Zusammenhang zu erschließen.
Vor der ersten Übung wird die Aufmerksamkeit auf das Merkkästchen gelenkt.

Have you got a good memory?
Diese Übung wird in Einzel- oder Partnerarbeit, mündlich und/oder schriftlich gemacht. Bei fortgeschritteneren Schülern kann sie schon nach dem zweiten Vortrag eingesetzt werden.

● Lösungen
- *He can make breakfast/do the washing/ironing/cooking himself.*
- *He can't get out of bed/wash his hair/clean the flat/get into his car himself.*
- *The Baileys can't do their shopping themselves.*

2. What problems do they have?
Im Klassenverband, in Einzel- oder Partnerarbeit, mündlich und/oder schriftlich werden die Lückentexte mithilfe der Bilder und unter Verwendung von Reflexivpronomen ausgefüllt.

● Lösungen
1. *She can't wash and comb her hair herself.*
2. *He can't get out of bed himself.*
3. *They can't do the cooking themselves.*
4. *They can't do the washing themselves.*
5. *He can't carry/lift his bag himself.*
6. *They can't get down themselves.*
7. *She can't stand up herself.*
8. *It can't open the door itself.*

3. Old people
Diese Übung knüpft an das Übung 1 einleitende Gespräch an:

L: *Earlier on we were talking about people who have difficulty doing things for themselves, weren't we? We've seen what sort of problems a handicapped person might have. Now let's think about old people. Do you know any old people who have difficulty doing things for themselves?*
(die Struktur ... *can't* ... *himself/herself/themselves* wird angeschrieben).

Nach einigen Schülerbeiträgen wird der Einführungstext von Übung 3 gelesen. In Partner- oder Gruppenarbeit schreiben die Lernenden ein paar Fragen auf, die man alleinstehenden alten Menschen oder alten Ehepaaren stellen könnte, um deren Probleme kennenzulernen. Dabei sollte auf die richtige Anwendung von *yourself* und *yourselves* geachtet werden.

● Vorschläge für Fragen
Can you get out of bed/do the washing/ironing/cooking/ cleaning/clean your flat/do your shopping/ ... yourself/yourselves?

4. Can you help?
In einem weiterführenden Schritt könnten die Lernenden überlegen, ob es in ihrer eigenen Umgebung Menschen gibt, die vielleicht Hilfe brauchen könnten. Neben Behinderten und alten Menschen wäre auch an andere Gruppen zu denken, z. B. an Heimkinder, Ausländer ohne Anschluss usw.

A 34

Das Stützwort one(s)

Das Stützwort *one* wird in der ersten und zweiten Übung wiederholt und geübt, die Pluralform *ones* in der dritten Übung.
Der Gebrauch des Stützwortes *one* wird vor der ersten Übung wie folgt in Erinnerung gerufen. Der Lehrer bringt einige Bilder von verschiedenen Städten oder bekannten

Sehenswürdigkeiten mit und fordert die Klasse auf, die Abbildungen zu lokalisieren:

L: *Let's see how good you are at geography. Look at this picture. Where do you think it is?*

S: *In …*

L: (Nach einigen Schülervorschlägen): *And this one? And this one?*

(Bemerkung: Nach *these/those* entfällt *ones: And these (pictures)?)*

1. Ann shows Mark her town

Die erste Übung stellt eine Art Rätseltext dar. Anhand der Stadtbeschreibung müssen die Gebäude richtig bezeichnet werden. Der Text kann zunächst mit dem Lernziel des *listening comprehension* vom Lehrer vorgelesen bzw. auf Hörkassette dargeboten werden. Gleichzeitig versuchen die Schüler, die Gebäude zu lokalisieren, ohne jedoch schon die Bezeichnungen in das Bild einzutragen.

2. Which one is it?

In Partnerarbeit befragen sich die Schüler gegenseitig über den Standort verschiedener Gebäude. Dazu muss der Text mehrmals still gelesen werden. Zur Demonstration der Arbeitsweise stellt der Lehrer die ersten Fragen der ganzen Klasse:

L: *Which building is the post office?* (Hilfestellungen: *The big one behind the park? The one with the flag?) Read the text and then tell me.*

S: *The one on the right of/next to the cinema.*

Danach stellt jeder Partner abwechselnd zwei Fragen zu Gebäuden, deren Standorte er selbst schon lokalisiert hat, z. B.:

1. *Which building is the hotel?*
2. *Which one is the bank?*

Antworten:

1. *The one next to/on the right of the restaurant/with the cars in front.*
2. *The big one on the corner/on the left of/next to the job centre.*

● Vorschläge für Fragen und Antworten

Which one is the

– *hospital?*	*The big one with the flag.*
– *department store?*	*The one on the corner.*
– *supermarket?*	*The long one in front of the hospital.*
– *police station?*	*The one between the railway station and the café.*
– *block of flats?*	*The tall/big one behind the park.*
– *sports centre?*	*The long/smaller one behind the park/on the right of the block of flats.*
– *café?*	*The one with the balcony/next to the police station.*
– *library?*	*The big one in front of the park.*
– *hotel?*	*The one with all the cars in front of it/next to the restaurant.*
– *restaurant?*	*The one between the library and the hotel/next to the library/hotel.*
– *cinema?*	*The one on the corner, opposite the station.*
– *post office?*	*The one next to the cinema.*
– *bank?*	*The big one opposite the library/next to the job centre.*
– *job centre?*	*The smaller one next to the bank.*

Anschließend werden in einem nächsten Schritt die Bezeichnungen der Gebäude in das Arbeitsblatt eingetragen.

Der Gebrauch von *one* kann abschließend zusammen mit den Lernenden erarbeitet werden, vgl. Merkkästchen.

Zur schriftlichen Festigung schreibt jeder Schüler drei Fragen nach dem folgenden Muster auf und reicht sie seinem Partner zur schriftlichen Beantwortung:

1. *Which building is the hotel?*
2. *Which one is the bank?*
3. *Which one is the sports centre?*

3. How much do you know about the world?

In dieser Übung wird die Pluralform *ones* wiederholt und geübt. In Partnerarbeit stellt Partner A die ersten vier Fragen *(Its cities);* Partner B stellt die vier folgenden *(Its countries).*

Its cities?

1. *Milan – Vienna*
2. *Nottingham – Belfast*
3. *Glasgow – Edinburgh*
4. *Cardiff – Bangor*

Its countries?

1. *Portugal – Greece*
2. *Switzerland – Nepal*
3. *Spain – Australia*
4. *Ireland – Bulgaria*

Zur weiteren Festigung der Struktur können die Schüler in Partner- bzw. Gruppenarbeit versuchen, nach folgendem Muster zwei ähnliche Fragen aufzuschreiben:

1. *Which of these (cities/countries/animals/ …)*
2. *Which ones …*

z. B. *Which of these animals lives in Asia/has fur/eats …?*
Which ones live in Australia/ …?

Zusätzlich zu den Fragen sind drei bis vier Antwortmöglichkeiten anzugeben, wovon zwei richtig sein müssen:

Which of these animals has fur? cat – elephant – cow – tiger
Which ones live in Germany? (cat – cow)

Die Fragen samt Antwortmöglichkeiten werden einer anderen Gruppe gestellt und von dieser beantwortet.